THE NATIONAL STRATEGY FOR

THE PHYSICAL PROTECTION
OF CRITICAL INFRASTRUCTURES
AND KEY ASSETS

FEBRUARY 2003

THE NATIONAL STRATEGY FOR

THE PHYSICAL PROTECTION OF CRITICAL INFRASTRUCTURES AND KEY ASSETS

FEBRUARY 2003

THE WHITE HOUSE
WASHINGTON

My Fellow Americans:

The September 11, 2001, attacks demonstrated the extent of our vulnerability to the terrorist threat. In the aftermath of these tragic events, we, as a Nation, have demonstrated firm resolve in protecting our critical infrastructures and key assets from further terrorist exploitation. In this effort, government at all levels, the private sector, and concerned citizens across the country have begun an important partnership and commitment to action.

To address the threat posed by those who wish to harm the United States, critical infrastructure owners and operators are assessing their vulnerabilities and increasing their investment in security. State and municipal governments across the country continue to take important steps to identify and assure the protection of key assets and services within their jurisdictions. Federal departments and agencies are working closely with industry to take stock of key assets and facilitate protective actions, while improving the timely exchange of important security-related information. The Office of Homeland Security is working closely with key public- and private-sector entities to implement the Homeland Security Advisory System across all levels of government and the critical sectors. Finally, I commend the Members of Congress for working diligently to pass comprehensive legislation that will unify our national critical infrastructure and key asset protection efforts in the new Department of Homeland Security.

Much work remains, however, to insure that we sustain these initial efforts over the long term. This *National Strategy for the Physical Protection of Critical Infrastructures and Key Assets* represents the first milestone in the road ahead. Consistent with the *National Strategy for Homeland Security*, this document identifies a clear set of goals and objectives and outlines the guiding principles that will underpin our efforts to secure the infrastructures and assets vital to our public health and safety, national security, governance, economy, and public confidence. It provides a unifying structure, defines roles and responsibilities, and identifies major initiatives that will drive our near-term protection priorities. Most importantly, it establishes a foundation for building and fostering a cooperative environment in which government, industry, and private citizens can work together to protect our critical infrastructures and key assets.

The *National Strategy for the Physical Protection of Critical Infrastructures and Key Assets* is the product of many months of consultation across a broad range of public- and private-sector stakeholders. It includes extensive input from the federal departments and agencies, state and municipal government, private-sector infrastructure owners and operators, the scientific and technology community, professional associations, research institutes, and concerned citizens across the country. This document is a truly national strategy.

As we work to implement this *Strategy*, it is important to remember that protection of our critical infrastructures and key assets is a shared responsibility. Accordingly, the success of our protective efforts will require close cooperation between government and the private sector at all levels. Each of us has an extremely important role to play in protecting the infrastructures and assets that are the basis for our daily lives and that represent important components of our national power and prestige.

The terrorist enemy that we face is highly determined, patient, and adaptive. In confronting this threat, protecting our critical infrastructures and key assets represents an enormous challenge. We must remain united in our resolve, tenacious in our approach, and harmonious in our actions to overcome this challenge and secure the foundations of our Nation and way of life.

TABLE OF CONTENTS

EXECUTIVE SUMMARY

This document defines the road ahead for a core mission area identified in the President's *National Strategy for Homeland Security*—reducing the Nation's vulnerability to acts of terrorism by protecting our critical infrastructures and key assets from physical attack.

This document, the *National Strategy for the Physical Protection of Critical Infrastructures and Key Assets*, the *Strategy*, identifies a clear set of national goals and objectives and outlines the guiding principles that will underpin our efforts to secure the infrastructures and assets vital to our national security, governance, public health and safety, economy, and public confidence. This *Strategy* also provides a unifying organization and identifies specific initiatives to drive our near-term national protection priorities and inform the resource allocation process. Most importantly, it establishes a foundation for building and fostering the cooperative environment in which government, industry, and private citizens can carry out their respective protection responsibilities more effectively and efficiently.

This *Strategy* recognizes the many important steps that public and private entities across the country have taken in response to the September 11, 2001, attacks to improve the security of their critical facilities, systems, and functions. Building upon these efforts, this document provides direction to the federal departments and agencies that have a role in critical infrastructure and key asset protection. It also suggests steps that state and local governments, private sector entities, and concerned citizens across America can take to enhance our collective infrastructure and asset security. In this light, this *Strategy* belongs and applies to the Nation as a whole, not just to the federal government or its constituent departments and agencies.

A New Mission

The September 11 attacks demonstrated our national-level physical vulnerability to the threat posed by a formidable enemy-focused, mass destruction terrorism. The events of that day also validated how determined, patient, and sophisticated—in both planning and execution—our terrorist enemies have become. The basic nature of our free society greatly enables terrorist operations and tactics, while, at the same time, hinders our ability to predict, prevent, or mitigate the effects of terrorist acts. Given these realities, it is imperative to develop a comprehensive national approach to physical protection.

Defining the End State: Strategic Objectives

The strategic objectives that underpin our national critical infrastructure and key asset protection effort include:

- Identifying and assuring the protection of those infrastructures and assets that we deem most critical in terms of national-level public health and safety, governance, economic and national security, and public confidence consequences;

- Providing timely warning and assuring the protection of those infrastructures and assets that face a specific, imminent threat; and

- Assuring the protection of other infrastructures and assets that may become terrorist targets over time by pursuing specific initiatives and enabling a collaborative environment in which federal, state, and local governments and the private sector can better protect the infrastructures and assets they control.

Homeland Security and Infrastructure Protection: A Shared Responsibility

Protecting America's critical infrastructures and key assets calls for a transition to a new national cooperative paradigm. The basic tenets of *homeland security* are fundamentally different from the historically defined tenets of national security. Traditionally, *national security* has been recognized largely as the responsibility of the federal government. *National security* is underpinned by the collective efforts of the military, foreign policy establishment, and intelligence community in the defense of our airspace and national borders, as well as operations overseas to protect our national interests.

Homeland security, particularly in the context of critical infrastructure and key asset protection, is a shared responsibility that cannot be accomplished by the federal government alone. It requires coordinated action on the part of federal, state, and local governments; the private sector; and concerned citizens across the country.[1]

THE CASE FOR ACTION

To build and implement a robust strategy to protect our critical infrastructures and key assets from further terrorist exploitation. we must understand the motivations of our enemies as well as their preferred tactics and targets. We must complement this understanding with a comprehensive assessment of the infrastructures and assets to be protected, their vulnerabilities, and the challenges associated with eliminating or mitigating those vulnerabilities—a task that will require the concerted efforts of our entire Nation.

The Importance of Critical Infrastructures

America's critical infrastructure sectors provide the foundation for our national security, governance. economic vitality, and way of life. Furthermore, their continued reliability, robustness, and resiliency create a sense of confidence and form an important part of our national identity and purpose. Critical infrastructures frame our daily lives and enable us to enjoy one of the highest overall standards of living in the world.

The facilities, systems, and functions that comprise our critical infrastructures are highly sophisticated and complex. They include human assets and physical and cyber systems that work together in processes that are highly interdependent. They also consist of key nodes that, in turn, are essential to the operation of the critical infrastructures in which they function.

The Importance of Key Assets

Key assets and high profile events are individual targets whose attack—in the worst-case scenarios—could result in not only large-scale human casualties and property destruction, but also profound damage to our national prestige, morale, and confidence.

Individually. key assets like nuclear power plants and dams may not be vital to the continuity of critical services at the national level. However, a successful strike against such targets may result in a significant loss of life and property in addition to long-term, adverse public health and safety consequences. Other key assets are symbolically equated with traditional American values and institutions or U.S. political and economic power. Our national icons. monuments, and historical attractions preserve history, honor achievements, and represent the natural grandeur of our country. They celebrate our American ideals and way of life and present attractive targets for terrorists, particularly when coupled with high profile events and celebratory activities that bring together significant numbers of people.

Understanding the Threat

Characteristics of Terrorism

The September 11 attacks on the World Trade Center and the Pentagon underscore the determination of our terrorist enemies. Terrorists are relentless and patient, as evidenced by their persistent targeting of the World Trade Center towers over the years. Terrorists are also opportunistic and flexible. They learn from experience and modify their tactics and targets to exploit perceived vulnerabilities and avoid observed strengths. As security increases around more predictable targets, they shift their focus to less protected assets. Enhancing countermeasures for any one terrorist tactic or target, therefore, makes it more likely that terrorists will favor another.

The Nature of Possible Attacks

Terrorists' pursuit of their long-term strategic objectives includes attacks on critical infrastructures and key assets. Terrorists target critical infrastructures to achieve three general types of effects:

- *Direct infrastructure effects:* Cascading disruption or arrest of the functions of critical infrastructures or key assets through direct attacks on a critical node, system, or function.

- *Indirect infrastructure effects:* Cascading disruption and financial consequences for government, society, and economy through public- and private-sector reactions to an attack.

- *Exploitation of infrastructure:* Exploitation of elements of a particular infrastructure to disrupt or destroy another target.

NATIONAL POLICY AND GUIDING PRINCIPLES

This *Strategy* reaffirms our longstanding national policy regarding critical infrastructure and key asset protection. It also delineates a set of guiding principles that will underpin our domestic protection strategy.

Statement of National Policy

As a Nation we remain committed to protecting our critical infrastructures and key assets from acts of terrorism that would:

- Impair the federal government's ability to perform essential national and homeland security missions and ensure the general public's health and safety;

- Undermine state and local government capacities to maintain order and to deliver minimum essential public services;

- Damage the private sector's capability to ensure the orderly functioning of the economy and the delivery of essential services; and

- Undermine the public's morale and confidence in our national economic and political institutions.

We must work collaboratively to employ the tools necessary to implement such protection.

Guiding Principles

Eight guiding principles underpin this *Strategy*:

- Assure public safety, public confidence, and services;

- Establish responsibility and accountability;

- Encourage and facilitate partnering among all levels of government and between government and industry;

- Encourage market solutions wherever possible and compensate for market failure with focused government intervention;

- Facilitate meaningful information sharing;

- Foster international cooperation;

- Develop technologies and expertise to combat terrorist threats; and

- Safeguard privacy and constitutional freedoms.

ORGANIZING AND PARTNERING FOR CRITICAL INFRASTRUCTURE AND KEY ASSET PROTECTION

Implementing this *Strategy* requires a unifying organization, a clear purpose, a common understanding of roles and responsibilities, accountability, and a set of well-understood coordinating processes. A solid organizational scheme sets the stage for effective engagement and interaction between the public and private sectors at all levels. Without it, the tasks of coordinating and integrating domestic protection policy, planning, resource allocation, performance measurement, and enabling initiatives across federal, state, and local governments and the private sector are virtually impossible to accomplish. Our strategy for action must provide the foundation these entities can use to achieve common objectives, applying their core capabilities, expertise, and experience as necessary to meet the threat at hand.

Federal Government Responsibilities

The federal government has the capacity to organize, convene, and coordinate broadly across governmental jurisdictions and the private sector. It has the responsibility to develop coherent national policies, strategies, and programs for implementation. In the context of homeland security, the federal government will coordinate the complementary efforts and capabilities of government and private institutions to raise our level of protection over the long term as appropriate for each of our critical infrastructures and key assets.

Every terrorist event has a potential national impact. The federal government will, therefore, take the lead to ensure that the three principal objectives detailed in the *Introduction* of this *Strategy* are met. This leadership role involves:

- Taking stock of our most critical facilities, systems, and functions and monitoring their preparedness across economic sectors and governmental jurisdictions;

- Assuring that federal, state, local, and private entities work together to protect critical facilities, systems, and functions that face an imminent threat and/or whose loss could have significant national consequences;

- Providing and coordinating national-level threat information, assessments, and warnings that are timely, actionable, and relevant to state, local, and private sector partners;

- Creating and implementing comprehensive, multi-tiered protection policies and programs;

- Exploring potential options for enablers and incentives to encourage stakeholders to devise solutions to their unique protection impediments;

- Developing cross-sector and cross-jurisdictional protection standards, guidelines, criteria, and protocols;

- Facilitating the sharing of critical infrastructure and key asset protection best practices and processes and vulnerability assessment methodologies;

- Conducting demonstration projects and pilot programs;

- Seeding the development and transfer of advanced technologies while taking advantage of private-sector expertise and competencies;

- Promoting national-level critical infrastructure and key asset protection education and awareness; and

- Improving the federal government's ability to work with state and local responders and service providers.

Federal Lead Departments and Agencies

The *National Strategy for Homeland Security* provides a sector-based organizational scheme for protecting critical infrastructure and key assets. It identifies the federal lead departments and agencies responsible for coordinating protection activities and developing and maintaining collaborative relationships with their state and local government and industry counterparts in the critical sectors.

In addition to securing federally owned and operated infrastructures and assets, the role of the federal lead departments and agencies is to assist state and local governments and private-sector partners in their efforts to:

- Organize and conduct protection and continuity of government and operations planning, and elevate awareness and understanding of threats and vulnerabilities to their critical facilities, systems, and functions;

- Identify and promote effective sector-specific protection practices and methodologies; and

- Expand voluntary security-related information sharing among private entities within the sector, as well as between government and private entities.

Department of Homeland Security

The Department of Homeland Security (DHS) will provide overall cross-sector coordination in this new organizational scheme, serving as the primary liaison and facilitator for cooperation among federal agencies, state and local governments, and the private sector. As the cross-sector coordinator, DHS will also be responsible for the detailed refinement and implementation of the core elements of this *Strategy*.

Other Federal Departments and Agencies

Besides the designated federal lead departments and agencies, the federal government will rely on the unique expertise of other departments and agencies to enhance the physical protection dimension of homeland security. Additionally, overall sector initiatives will often include an international component or requirement, require the development of a coordinated relationship with other governments or agencies, and entail information sharing with foreign governments. Accordingly, the Department of State (DoS) will support the development and implementation of sector protection initiatives by laying the groundwork for bilateral and multilateral infrastructure protective agreements with our international allies.

State and Local Government Responsibilities

The 50 states, 4 territories, and 87,000 local jurisdictions that comprise this Nation have an important and unique role to play in the protection of our critical infrastructures and key assets. State and local governments, like the federal government, should identify and secure the critical infrastructures and key assets they own and operate within their jurisdictions.

States should also engender coordination of protective and emergency response activities and resource support among local jurisdictions and regions in close collaboration with designated federal lead departments and agencies. States should further facilitate coordinated planning and preparedness for critical infrastructure and key asset protection, applying unified criteria for determining criticality, prioritizing protection investments, and exercising preparedness within their jurisdictions. States should also act as conduits for requests for federal assistance when the threat at hand exceeds the capabilities of local jurisdictions and private entities within those jurisdictions. Finally, states should facilitate the exchange of relevant security information and threat alerts down to the local level.

State and local governments look to the federal government for coordination, support, and resources when national requirements exceed local capabilities. Protecting critical infrastructures and key assets will require a close and extensive cooperation among all three levels of government. DHS, in particular, is designed to provide a single point of coordination with state and local governments for homeland security issues, including the critical infrastructure and key asset protection mission area. Other federal lead departments and agencies and law enforcement organizations will provide support as needed and appropriate for specific critical infrastructure and key asset protection requirements.

Private Sector Responsibilities

The lion's share of our critical infrastructures and key assets are owned and operated by the private sector. Customarily, private sector firms prudently engage in risk management planning and invest in security as a necessary function of business operations and customer confidence. Moreover, in the present threat environment, the private sector generally remains the first line of defense for its own facilities. Consequently, private-sector owners and operators should reassess and adjust their planning, assurance, and investment programs to better accommodate the increased risk presented by deliberate acts of violence. Since the events of

September 11, many businesses have increased their threshold investments and undertaken enhancements in security in an effort to meet the demands of the new threat environment.

For most enterprises, the level of investment in security reflects implicit risk-versus-consequence tradeoffs, which are based on: (1) what is known about the risk environment; and (2) what is economically justifiable and sustainable in a competitive marketplace or in an environment of limited government resources. Given the dynamic nature of the terrorist threat and the severity of the consequences associated with many potential attack scenarios, the private sector naturally looks to the government for better information to help make its crucial security investment decisions.

Similarly, the private sector looks to the government for assistance when the threat at hand exceeds an enterprise's capability to protect itself beyond a reasonable level of additional investment. In this light, the federal government will collaborate with the private sector (and state and local governments) to assure the protection of nationally critical infrastructures and assets; provide timely warning and assure the protection of infrastructures and assets that face a specific, imminent threat; and promote an environment in which the private sector can better carry out its specific protection responsibilities.

Near-term Roadmap: Cross-Sector Security Priorities

The issues and security initiatives outlined in the *Cross-Sector Security Priorities* chapter of this document represent important, near-term national priorities. They are focused on impediments to physical protection that significantly impact multiple sectors of our government, society, and economy. Potential solutions to the problems identified—such as information sharing and threat indications and warning—are high-leverage areas that, when realized, will enhance the Nation's collective ability to protect critical infrastructures and key assets across the board. Accordingly, DHS and designated federal lead departments and agencies will prepare detailed implementation plans to support the activities outlined in this chapter.

This *Strategy* identifies major cross-sector initiatives in five areas:

Planning and Resource Allocation: This *Strategy* identifies eight major initiatives in this area.

- Create collaborative mechanisms for government-industry critical infrastructure and key asset protection planning;

- Identify key protection priorities and develop appropriate supporting mechanisms for these priorities;

- Foster increased sharing of risk-management expertise between the public and private sectors;

- Identify options for incentives for private organizations that proactively implement enhanced security measures;

- Coordinate and consolidate federal and state protection plans;

- Establish a task force to review legal impediments to reconstitution and recovery in the aftermath of an attack against a critical infrastructure or key asset;

- Develop an integrated critical infrastructure and key asset geospatial database; and

- Conduct critical infrastructure protection planning with our international partners.

Information Sharing and Indications and Warnings: This *Strategy* identifies six major initiatives in this area.

- Define protection-related information sharing requirements and establish effective, efficient information sharing processes;

- Implement the statutory authorities and powers of the *Homeland Security Act of 2002* to protect security and proprietary information regarded as sensitive by the private sector;

- Promote the development and operation of critical sector Information Sharing Analysis Centers;

- Improve processes for domestic threat data collection, analysis, and dissemination to state and local government and private industry;

- Support the development of interoperable secure communications systems for state and local governments and designated private sector entities; and

- Complete implementation of the Homeland Security Advisory System.

Personnel Surety, Building Human Capital, and Awareness: This *Strategy* identifies six major initiatives in this area.

- Coordinate the development of national standards for personnel surety;

- Develop a certification program for background-screening companies;

- Explore establishment of a certification regime or model security training program for private security officers;

- Identify requirements and develop programs to protect critical personnel;

- Facilitate the sharing of public- and private-sector protection expertise; and

- Develop and implement a national awareness program for critical infrastructure and key asset protection.

Technology and Research & Development: This *Strategy* identifies four major initiatives in this area.

- Coordinate public- and private-sector security research and development activities;

- Coordinate interoperability standards to ensure compatibility of communications systems;

- Explore methods to authenticate and verify personnel identity; and

- Improve technical surveillance, monitoring and detection capabilities.

Modeling, Simulation, and Analysis: This *Strategy* identifies seven major initiatives in this area.

- Enable the integration of modeling, simulation, and analysis into national infrastructure and asset protection planning and decision support activities;

- Develop economic models of near- and long-term effects of terrorist attacks;

- Develop critical node/chokepoint and interdependency analysis capabilities;

- Model interdependencies across sectors with respect to conflicts between sector alert and warning procedures and actions;

- Conduct integrated risk modeling of cyber and physical threats, vulnerabilities, and consequences; and

- Develop models to improve information integration.

Unique Protection Areas

In addition to the cross-sector themes addressed in this *Strategy*, the individual critical infrastructure sectors

and special categories of key assets have unique issues that require action. These considerations and associated enabling initiatives are discussed in the last two chapters of this *Strategy*.

Securing Critical Infrastructures: This *Strategy* identifies major protection initiatives for the following critical infrastructure sectors:

- Agriculture and Food

- Water

- Public Health

- Emergency Services

- Defense Industrial Base

- Telecommunications

- Energy

- Transportation

- Banking and Finance

- Chemicals and Hazardous Materials

- Postal and Shipping

Protecting Key Assets: This *Strategy* identifies major protection initiatives for the following key asset categories:

- National Monuments and Icons

- Nuclear Power Plants

- Dams

- Government Facilities

- Commercial Key Assets

---

1   The *National Strategy for Homeland Security* defines "State" to mean "any state of the United States, the District of Columbia, Puerto Rico, the Virgin Islands, Guam, American Samoa, the Commonwealth of the Northern Mariana Islands, or the trust territory of the Pacific Islands." The *Strategy* defines "local government" as "any county, city, village, town, district, or other political subdivision of any state, any Native American tribe or authorized tribal organization, or Alaska native village or organization, and includes any rural community or unincorporated town or village or any other public entity for which and application for assistance is made by a state or political subdivision thereof."

INTRODUCTION

On July 16, 2002, President Bush issued the *National Strategy for Homeland Security*, an overarching strategy for mobilizing and organizing our Nation to secure the U.S. homeland from terrorist attacks. It communicates a comprehensive approach "based on the principles of shared responsibility and partnership with Congress, state and local governments, the private sector, and the American people"—a truly <u>national</u> effort, not merely a federal one.

The *National Strategy for Homeland Security* defines "homeland security" and identifies a strategic framework based on three national objectives. In order of priority, these are: (1) preventing terrorist attacks within the United States, (2) reducing America's vulnerability to terrorism, and (3) minimizing the damage and recovering from attacks that do occur.

HOMELAND SECURITY CRITICAL MISSION AREAS

Intelligence and Warning

Border and Transportation Security

Domestic Counter-terrorism

Protecting Critical Infrastructures and Key Assets

Defending against Catastrophic Terrorism

Emergency Preparedness and Response

To attain these objectives, the *National Strategy for Homeland Security* aligns our homeland security efforts into six critical mission areas: intelligence and warning, border and transportation security, domestic counter-terrorism, protecting critical infrastructures and key assets, defending against catastrophic terrorism, and emergency preparedness and response.

This document, the *National Strategy for the Physical Protection of Critical Infrastructures and Key Assets*, the *Strategy*,[1] takes the next step to facilitate the strategic planning process for a core mission area identified in

"The United States will forge an unprecedented level of cooperation throughout all levels of government, with private industry and institutions, and with the American people to protect our critical infrastructure and key assets from terrorist attack."

- The National Strategy for Homeland Security

the *National Strategy for Homeland Security*—reducing the Nation's vulnerability by protecting our critical infrastructures and key assets from physical attack. It identifies a clear set of national goals and objectives and outlines the guiding principles that will underpin our efforts to secure the infrastructures and assets vital to our national security, governance, public health and safety, economy, and public confidence. It also provides a unifying organizational structure and identifies specific initiatives to drive our near-term national protection priorities and inform the resource allocation process. Most importantly, it provides a foundation for building and fostering the cooperative environment in which government, industry, and private citizens can carry out their respective protection responsibilities more effectively and efficiently.

This *Strategy* recognizes the many important steps that public and private entities across the country have taken in response to the World Trade Center and Pentagon attacks on September 11, 2001, to improve the security of their critical facilities, systems, and functions. Building on these efforts, this *Strategy* provides direction to the federal departments and agencies that have a role in critical infrastructure and key asset protection. It also suggests steps that state and local governments, private sector entities, and concerned citizens across America can take to enhance our collective infrastructure and asset security. Accordingly, this *Strategy* belongs and applies to the Nation as a whole, not just to the federal government or its constituent departments and agencies.

This *Strategy* complements the *National Strategy to Secure Cyberspace*, which focuses on the identification, assessment, and protection of interconnected information systems and networks. The *Physical and Cyber Strategies* share common underlying policy objectives and principles. Together, they form the road ahead for one of our core homeland security mission areas.

A NEW MISSION

The September 11 attacks on the World Trade Center and the Pentagon demonstrated our national-level physical vulnerability to the threat posed by a formidable enemy—focused, mass destruction terrorism. The events of that day also validated how determined, patient, and sophisticated—in both planning and execution—our terrorist enemies have become. Ironically, the basic nature of our free society greatly enables terrorist operations and tactics, while, at the same time, it hinders our ability to predict, prevent, or mitigate the effects of terrorist acts. Given these

realities, it is imperative to develop a comprehensive national approach to physical protection.

Protecting America's critical infrastructures and key assets represents an enormous challenge. Our Nation's critical infrastructures and key assets are a highly complex, heterogeneous, and interdependent mix of facilities, systems, and functions that are vulnerable to a wide variety of threats. Their sheer numbers, pervasiveness, and interconnected nature create an almost infinite array of high-payoff targets for terrorist exploitation. Given the immense size and scope of the potential target set, we cannot assume that we will be able to protect completely all things at all times against all conceivable threats. As we develop protective measures for one particular type of target, our terrorist enemies will likely focus on another. To be effective, our national protection strategy must be based on a thorough understanding of these complexities as we build and implement a focused plan for action.

DEFINING THE END STATE: STRATEGIC OBJECTIVES

To frame the initial focus of our national protection effort, we must acknowledge that the assets, systems, and functions that comprise our infrastructure sectors are not uniformly "critical" in nature, particularly in a national or major regional context.

The **first** objective of this *Strategy* is to identify and assure the protection of those assets, systems, and functions that we deem most "critical" in terms of national-level public health and safety, governance, economic and national security, and public confidence. We must develop a comprehensive, prioritized assessment of facilities, systems, and functions of national-level criticality and monitor their preparedness across infrastructure sectors. The federal government will work closely with state and local governments and the private sector to establish a uniform methodology for determining national-level criticality. This methodology will enable a focus on high-priority activities and the development of consistent approaches to counter the terrorist threat.

The **second** major objective is to assure the protection of infrastructures and assets that face a specific, imminent threat. Federal, state, and local governments and private-sector partners must collaborate closely to develop thorough assessment and alert processes and systems to ensure that threatened assets receive timely advance warnings. These entities must further cooperate to provide focused protection against the anticipated threat.

Finally, as we act to secure our most critical infrastructures and assets, we must remain cognizant that criticality varies as a function of time, risk, and market changes. Acting to better secure our highest priority facilities, systems, and functions, we should expect our terrorist enemies to shift their destructive focus to targets they consider less protected and more likely to yield desired shock effects. Hence, the third objective of this *Strategy* is to pursue collaborative measures and initiatives to assure the protection of other potential targets that may become attractive over time. The focus will be to foster an environment in which key public- and private-sector stakeholders can better protect the infrastructures and assets they control according to their specific responsibilities, competencies, and capabilities.

The last three chapters of this *Strategy* detail the cross-sector and sector-specific priority solution paths we will pursue to achieve the fullest measure of national protection possible across all categories of critical infrastructures and key assets.

HOMELAND SECURITY AND INFRASTRUCTURE PROTECTION: A SHARED RESPONSIBILITY

Protecting America's critical infrastructures and key assets calls for a transition to an important new national cooperative paradigm. The basic tenets of *homeland* security are fundamentally different from the historically defined tenets of *national* security. Historically, securing the United States entailed the projection of force outside of our borders. We protected ourselves by "keeping our neighborhood safe" in the global, geopolitical sense. The capability and responsibility to carry out this mission rested largely with the federal government.

The emergence of international terrorism within our borders has moved the front line of domestic security to Main Street, U.S.A. Faced with the realities of the September 11 attacks, the mission of protecting our homeland now entails "keeping our neighborhood safe" in the most literal sense. Safeguarding our Nation against the terrorist threat depends on our ability to marshal and project appropriate resources inward. Respect for the open, pluralistic nature of our society; the individual rights and liberties of our citizenry; and our federalist system of government define the framework within which security can be implemented.

Acting alone, the federal government lacks the comprehensive set of tools and competencies required

"Homeland security is a concerted national effort to prevent terrorist attacks within the United States, reduce America's vulnerability to terrorism, and minimize the damage and recover from attacks that do occur."

- The National Strategy for Homeland Security

to deliver the most effective protection and response for most homeland security threats. Therefore, to combat the threat terrorism poses for our critical infrastructures and key assets, we must draw upon the resources and capabilities of those who stand on the new front lines—our local communities and private sector entities that comprise our national critical infrastructure sectors.

Forging this unprecedented level of cooperation will require dramatic changes in the institutional mindsets honed and shaped by Cold War-era regimes. Success in this effort must be built and sustained over time. This *Strategy* provides a starting point for defining how this national-level cooperation can best be achieved.

In the context of a new national cooperative paradigm, this *Strategy* further serves as an important vehicle for educating the public and achieving realistic expectations on the emergent terrorist threat and the roles government and industry must play in defending against it. Public understanding and acceptance of this *Strategy* is essential. The American public's resilience and support will be sustainable in the aftermath of future terrorist attacks only if expectations are clearly defined, attainable, and fulfilled.

STRATEGY OVERVIEW

This *Strategy* is comprehensive in scope and focused in detail. The following chapters lay out a roadmap to identify specific priority actions to be taken to assure more comprehensive protection of our critical infrastructures and key assets.

The Case for Action

This chapter discusses the role critical infrastructures and key assets play as a foundation of our Nation's economic security, governance, national defense, public health and safety, and public confidence. It describes in greater detail the characteristics of terrorism and the challenges we must

address to protect the Nation's critical infrastructures and key assets against this threat.

National Policy and Guiding Principles

This chapter describes the overarching national policy and guiding principles that underpin this *Strategy* and our collective approach to action.

Organizing and Partnering for Critical Infrastructure and Key Asset Protection

This chapter provides an organizational structure for our national-level critical infrastructure and key asset protection effort. It also clarifies key public- and private-sector roles and responsibilities and provides a collaborative framework for cross-sector and cross-jurisdictional infrastructure and asset protection.

Cross-Sector Security Priorities

This chapter addresses important cross-sector issues, impediments to action, and the steps necessary to address them. It describes actions to foster cooperation, lower costs, and provide leverage across key issue areas for maximum effect. In concert, these initiatives form the framework through which we will align the resources of the federal budget to the critical infrastructure and key asset protection mission.

Securing Critical Infrastructures

This chapter outlines protection priorities for the critical infrastructure sectors identified in the *National Strategy for Homeland Security*. The overviews provided are designed to highlight pressing issues in need of concerted attention at the individual sector level. Each federal lead department and agency will develop plans and programs to implement or facilitate these priority sector initiatives.

Protecting Key Assets

This chapter describes protection considerations for unique facilities, such as dams, nuclear power plants, and national monuments and icons whose attack, in a worst-case scenario, could present significant health and safety and/or public confidence consequences.

Conclusion

This chapter summarizes the next steps required to assure comprehensive protection of our critical infrastructures and key assets.

---

1   The primary focus of this *Strategy* is the physical protection of critical infrastructures and key assets. The protective strategy for information technology and network assets for specific sectors is discussed in detail in the *National Strategy to Secure Cyberspace*. Accordingly, the protection of the Information Technology component of the Information and Telecommunications sector is not discussed in this document.

THE CASE FOR ACTION

Developing an effective strategy for critical infrastructure and key asset protection requires a clear understanding of the threats we face and the potential consequences they entail. The September 11 attacks were a wake-up call. Before these devastating events, we, as Americans, considered ourselves relatively immune to a massive physical attack on our homeland. Our victory in the Cold War left us with few significant conventional military threats, and the world of terrorism seemed more the concern of troubled regions like the Middle East than Middle America. As a Nation, we were generally unfamiliar with the motivations of terrorists and the deep hatred behind their agendas. Furthermore, we underestimated the depth and scope of their capabilities and did not fully appreciate the extent to which they would go to carry out their destructive acts. The September 11 attacks changed these misconceptions.

Al-Qaeda terrorists exploited key elements of our own transportation infrastructure as weapons. Their targets were key assets symbolic of our national prestige and military and economic power. The effects of the attacks cascaded throughout our society, economy, and government. As a Nation, we became suddenly and painfully aware of the extent of our domestic vulnerability—more so than at any time since the Second World War.

To protect our critical infrastructures and key assets from further terrorist exploitation, we must understand the intent and objectives of terrorism as well as the tactics and techniques its agents could employ against various types of targets. We must complement this understanding with a comprehensive assessment of the assets to be protected, their vulnerabilities, and the challenges associated with eliminating or mitigating those vulnerabilities—a task that will require the concerted efforts of our entire Nation.

THE SIGNIFICANCE OF CRITICAL INFRASTRUCTURES AND KEY ASSETS

The Importance of Critical Infrastructures

America's critical infrastructure sectors provide the goods and services that contribute to a strong national defense and thriving economy. Moreover, their continued reliability, robustness, and resiliency create a sense of confidence and form an important part of our national identity and strategic purpose. They also frame our way of life and enable Americans to enjoy one of the highest overall standards of living of any country in the world.

When we flip a switch, we expect light. When we pick up a phone, we expect a dial tone. When we turn a tap, we expect drinkable water. Electricity, clean water, and telecommunications are only a few of the critical infrastructure services that we tend to take for granted. They have become so basic in our daily lives that we notice them only when, for some reason, service is disrupted. When disruption does occur, we expect reasonable explanations and speedy restoration of service.

The *National Strategy for Homeland Security* categorizes our critical infrastructures into the following sectors:

CRITICAL INFRASTRUCTURE SECTORS

Agriculture

Food

Water

Public Health

Emergency Services

Government

Defense Industrial Base

Information and Telecommunications

Energy

Transportation

Banking and Finance

Chemical Industry and Hazardous Materials

Postal and Shipping

Critical infrastructures are "systems and assets, whether physical or virtual, so vital to the United States that the incapacity or destruction of such systems and assets would have a debilitating impact on security, national economic security, national public health or safety, or any combination of those matters."

– USA Patriot Act

Together these industries provide:

Production and Delivery of Essential Goods and Services
Critical infrastructure sectors such as agriculture, food, and water, along with public health and emergency services, provide the essential goods and services that Americans depend on to survive.

Energy, transportation, banking and financial services, chemical manufacturing, postal services, and shipping sustain the Nation's economy and make possible and available a continuous array of goods and services.

Interconnectedness and Operability
Information and telecommunications infrastructures connect and increasingly control the operations of other critical infrastructures.

Public Safety and Security
Our government institutions guarantee our national security, freedom, and governance, as well as services that make up the Nation's public safety net.

The facilities, systems, and functions that comprise our critical infrastructures are highly sophisticated and complex. They consist of human capital and physical and cyber systems that work together in processes that are highly interdependent. They each encompass a series of key nodes that are, in turn, essential to the operation of the critical infrastructures in which they function. To complicate matters further, our most critical infrastructures typically interconnect and, therefore, depend on the continued availability and operation of other dynamic systems and functions.

For example, e-commerce depends on electricity as well as information and communications. Assuring electric service requires operational transportation and distribution systems to guarantee the delivery of fuel necessary to generate power. Such interdependencies

have developed over time and are the product of innovative operational processes that have fueled unprecedented efficiency and productivity. Given the dynamic nature of these interdependent infrastructures and the extent to which our daily lives rely on them, a successful terrorist attack to disrupt or destroy them could have tremendous impact beyond the immediate target and continue to reverberate long after the immediate damage is done.

The Importance of Key Assets

Key assets represent individual targets whose destruction could cause large-scale injury, death, or destruction of property, and/or profoundly damage our national prestige, and confidence. Such assets and activities alone may not be vital to the continuity of critical services on a national scale, but an attack on any one of them could produce, in the worst case, significant loss of life and/or public health and safety consequences. This category includes such facilities as nuclear power plants, dams, and hazardous materials storage facilities.

Other key assets are symbolically equated with traditional American values and institutions or U.S. political and economic power. Our national symbols, icons, monuments, and historical attractions preserve history, honor achievements, and represent the natural grandeur of our country. They also celebrate our American ideals and way of life—a key target of terrorist attacks. Successful terrorist strikes against such assets could profoundly impact national public confidence. Monuments and icons, furthermore, tend to be gathering places for large numbers of people, particularly during high-profile celebratory events—a factor that adds to their attractiveness as targets.

Ownership of key assets varies. The private sector owns and operates dams and nuclear power plants as well as most of this Nation's large buildings holding important commercial and/or symbolic value and/or housing large numbers of people. The protection of national monuments and icons often entails overlapping state, local, and federal jurisdictions. Some are managed and operated by private foundations. These realities complicate our protective efforts.

UNDERSTANDING THE THREAT

Characteristics of Terrorism

The September 11 attacks offered undeniable proof that our critical infrastructures and key assets represent high-value targets for terrorism. The attacks underscored the determination and patience of our terrorist enemies. The highly coordinated nature of the strikes demonstrated a previously unanticipated level of sophistication in terms of planning and execution. Through these attacks, Al-Qaeda terrorists also showed a dogged resolve in pursuit of their objectives. When their first attempt to topple the World Trade Center towers failed in 1993, they persisted by planning and executing a second attack eight years later that proved to be more successful than even they expected.

Our terrorist enemies have proven themselves to be opportunistic and flexible. As illustrated by the two separate World Trade Center attacks, they learn from experience and modify their tactics accordingly. They also adapt their methods in order to exploit newly observed or perceived vulnerabilities. As security increases around more predictable targets, they will likely seek more accessible and less protected facilities and events. Enhancing countermeasures against any one terrorist tactic, therefore, makes it more likely that terrorists will favor another.

Terrorists are inventive and resourceful in terms of target selection, as well as in the selection and use of specific instruments of violence and intimidation. They exploit vulnerabilities wherever they exist, with any means at their disposal, at times and locations of their choosing. Terrorists are attempting to acquire a broad range of weapons, from high-yield conventional explosives and firearms to weapons of mass destruction. Oftentimes the nature of the target will dictate the weapon of choice. Other times the availability of a particular type of weapon, such as a nuclear or biological device, will determine target selection. The matching of means to ends is limited only by the creativity and resources of the terrorists; the only constant is their desire to inflict maximum destruction, injury, and shock in pursuit of their strategic objectives.

Terrorism is with us for the foreseeable future. Following the September 11 attacks, President Bush stated that the war on terrorism would be a long-term effort. While the tools and tactics of terrorists may change, their fundamental determination remains the same. Those with enmity toward the U.S. and its interests consider terrorism an effective weapon to use against us, and they will continue to employ such tactics until we can prove that it is not.

The Nature of Possible Attacks

The terrorist endgame includes a complex mix of political, economic, and psychological objectives. To achieve their objectives, terrorists may choose to target critical infrastructures and key assets as low-risk means to generate mass casualties, shock, and panic.

Terrorists target critical infrastructure and key assets to achieve effects that fall into three general categories:

- *Direct infrastructure effects:* Cascading disruption or arrest of the functions of critical infrastructures or key assets through direct attacks on a critical node, system, or function.

  The immediate damage to facilities and disruption of services that resulted from the attack on the World Trade Center towers, which housed critical assets of the financial services sector, are examples of direct infrastructure effects.

- *Indirect infrastructure effects:* Cascading disruption and financial consequences for government, society, and economy through public- and private-sector reactions to an attack.

  Public disengagement from air travel and other facets of the economy as a result of the September 11 attacks exemplifies this effect. Mitigating the potential consequences from these types of attacks will require careful assessment of policy and regulatory responses, understanding the psychology of their impacts, and appropriately weighing the costs and benefits of specific actions in response to small-scale attacks.

- *Exploitation of infrastructure:* Exploitation of elements of a particular infrastructure to disrupt or destroy another target.

  On September 11, terrorists exploited elements of the aviation infrastructure to attack the World Trade Center and the Pentagon, which represented seats of U.S. economic and military power. Determining the potential cascading and cross-sector consequences of this type of attack is extremely difficult.

CHALLENGES TO PROTECTING CRITICAL INFRASTRUCTURES AND KEY ASSETS

The New Front Lines

Our technologically sophisticated society and institutions present a wide array of potential targets for terrorist exploitation. Our critical infrastructure industries change rapidly to reflect the demands of the markets they serve. Much of the expertise required for planning and taking action to protect critical infrastructures and key assets lies outside the federal government, including precise knowledge of what needs to be protected. In effect, the front lines of defense in this new type of battle have moved into our communities and the individual institutions that make up our critical infrastructure sectors.

Private industry owns and operates approximately 85 percent of our critical infrastructures and key assets. Facility operators have always been responsible for protecting their physical assets against unauthorized intruders. These measures, however conventionally effective, generally have not been designed to cope with significant military or terrorist threats, or the cascading economic and psychological impact they may entail.

The unique characteristics of critical infrastructures and key assets, their continuing—often rapid—evolution, and the significant impediments complicating their protection will require an unprecedented level of key public- and private-sector cooperation and coordination. Our country has more than 87,000 jurisdictions of local governance alone. The challenge ahead is to develop a coordinated and complementary system that reinforces protection efforts rather than duplicates them, and that meets mutually identified essential requirements. In addition, many of our critical infrastructures also span national borders and, therefore, must be protected within the context of international cooperation.

A NEW PARADIGM: COOPERATION AND PARTNERSHIP

Our open society, highly creative and responsive economic markets, and system of values that engenders individual recognition and freedom have created wealth for our nation, built a strong national security system, and instilled a sense of national confidence in the future. Destruction of our traditions, values, and way of life represents a key objective of our terrorist enemies. Ironically, the tenets of American society that make us free also create an environment that facilitates terrorist operations.

As we strive to understand the nature of terrorism and identify appropriate means to defend against it, we will require new collaborative structures and mechanisms for working together. During the Cold War era, many government and private organizations isolated parts of their physical and information infrastructures into "stovepipes" to assure their protection. This approach is no longer adequate to protect our homeland from determined terrorists. Stimulating voluntary, rapidly adaptive protection activities requires a culture of trust and ongoing collaboration among relevant public- and private-sector stakeholders, rather than more traditional systems of command and control.

Security investments made by all levels of government and private industry have increased since the September 11 attacks. As terrorism continues to evolve, so must the way in which we protect our

country and ourselves. The costs of protection—including expenditures to develop new technologies, tools, and procedures—will weigh heavily on all levels of government and private industry. Consequently, an effective protection strategy must incorporate well-planned and highly coordinated approaches that have been developed by the best minds in our country through innovation and sharing of information, best practices, and shared resources.

National Resilience: Sustaining Protection for the Long Term

Combating terrorism will be a long-term effort. Its dynamic nature means that we must enhance the protection of our critical infrastructures and key assets in an environment of persistent and evolving threats.

Our Nation's critical infrastructures are generally robust and resilient. These attributes result from decades of experience gained from responding to natural disasters, such as hurricanes and floods, and the deliberate acts of malicious individuals. The critical infrastructure sectors have learned from each disruption and applied those lessons to improve their protection, response, and recovery operations. For example, during the immediate aftermath of the September 11 attacks, the electric system in New York City remained operational for the island of Manhattan outside of the World Trade Center complex—Ground Zero. Furthermore, needed electric service at Ground Zero was quickly and efficiently restored to support rescue and recovery operations. This success is a good example of American ingenuity, as well as a tenacious application of lessons learned from the 1993 World Trade Center bombing and other terrorist events.

Resilience is characteristic of most U.S. communities, and it is reflected in the ways they cope with natural disasters. Over time, residents of communities in areas that are persistently subjected to natural disasters become accustomed to what to expect when one occurs. Institutions and residents in such areas grow to understand the nature of catastrophic events, as well as their roles and responsibilities in managing their after-effects. They are also familiar with and rely on trusted community systems and resources that are in place to support protection, response, and recovery efforts. As a result, they have confidence in their communities' abilities to contend with the aftermath of disasters and learn from each event.

Institutions and residents nationwide must likewise come to understand the nature of terrorism, its consequences, and the role they play in combating it. Ideally, they will become familiar with and have confidence in

THE PROTECTION CHALLENGE

Agriculture and Food	1,912,000 farms; 87,000 food-processing plants
Water	1,800 federal reservoirs; 1,600 municipal waste water facilities
Public Health	5,800 registered hospitals
Emergency Services	87,000 U.S. localities
Defense Industrial Base	250,000 firms in 215 distinct industries
Telecommunications	2 billion miles of cable
Energy	
Electricity	2,800 power plants
Oil and Natural Gas	300,000 producing sites
Transportation	
Aviation	5,000 public airports
Passenger Rail and Railroads	120,000 miles of major railroads
Highways, Trucking, and Busing	590,000 highway bridges
Pipelines	2 million miles of pipelines
Maritime	300 inland/costal ports
Mass Transit	500 major urban public transit operators
Banking and Finance	26,600 FDIC insured institutions
Chemical Industry and Hazardous Materials	66,000 chemical plants
Postal and Shipping	137 million delivery sites
Key Assets	
National Monuments and Icons	5,800 historic buildings
Nuclear Power Plants	104 commercial nuclear power plants
Dams	80,000 dams
Government Facilities	3,000 government owned/operated facilities
Commercial Assets	460 skyscrapers

*These are approximate figures.

the protection, response, and recovery mechanisms that exist within their communities. Together with local officials, private organizations and residents must work to improve these systems and resources to meet the challenge of safeguarding our country from terrorists.

Our challenge is to identify, build upon, and apply the lessons learned from the September 11 attacks to anticipate and protect against future terrorist attacks on our critical infrastructures and key assets. Our ability to do so will determine how successfully we adapt to the current dynamic threat environment and whether we can emerge as a stronger, more vibrant nation with our values and way of life intact.

NATIONAL POLICY AND GUIDING PRINCIPLES

STATEMENT OF NATIONAL POLICY

This document reaffirms our Nation's longstanding policy regarding critical infrastructure and key asset protection. It also delineates a set of guiding principles that underpins our strategy for action to protect our Nation's critical infrastructures and key assets from terrorist attack.

As a Nation, we are committed to protecting our critical infrastructures and key assets from acts of terrorism that would:

- Impair the federal government's ability to perform essential national security missions and ensure the general public's health and safety;

- Undermine state and local government capacities to maintain order and to deliver minimum essential public services;

- Damage the private sector's capability to ensure the orderly functioning of the economy and the delivery of essential services; and

- Undermine the public's morale and confidence in our national economic and political institutions.

As a Nation, we must utilize every tool at our disposal and work collaboratively to develop and implement the protective measures that this policy entails. The strategic objectives discussed in the *Introduction* will focus and drive this effort.

GUIDING PRINCIPLES

Our domestic protection efforts are grounded in core strengths and values that we have traditionally relied upon during major periods of crisis in our Nation's history. Using these core strengths and values as a guide, eight principles underpin this *Strategy* and its associated enabling initiatives:

1. Assure public safety, public confidence, and services

Anticipating that widespread or large-scale disruptions will undermine public confidence in our political and economic institutions, terrorists will continue to use horrific violence against people and property to impact the efficient functioning of our

society and economy. By making strategic improvements in security and reducing the vulnerability of our Nation's critical infrastructures and key assets to such physical attack—particularly those involving the most catastrophic potential consequences—this strategy seeks to reassure the public and reinforce its confidence in our institutions and systems.

By making our infrastructures and key assets more robust through such measures as deliberate redundancies, hardening, and dispersal, we increase their capacity to withstand attack without sustaining significant damage. Through effective protection and response planning, we make them more resilient to allow for the quick restoration of critical services to minimize the detrimental effects to our economy and public welfare. Implementing and exercising well-developed plans assures their effectiveness in times of crisis and is key to shaping public expectations and instilling confidence in our Nation's ability to manage the aftermath of terrorist attacks.

2. Establish responsibility and accountability

This *Strategy* recognizes the crucial role of government, industry, and the public at large in protecting our critical infrastructures and key assets from terrorist attack. Our valued heritage of federalism and limited government decentralizes our governance and affords private citizens and institutions with certain rights and freedoms to conduct their lives and businesses. In this context, organizations and individuals outside of the federal government must take the lead in many aspects of critical infrastructure and key asset protection.

Consequently, a key component of this *Strategy* is the delineation of roles, responsibilities, and accountability among the various public- and private-sector entities that have an important part to play in domestic protection. This necessarily encompasses the mechanisms required to coordinate and integrated protection policies, planning, resource management, performance measurement, and enabling initiatives across federal, state, and local governments and the private sector.

3. Encourage and facilitate partnering among all levels of government and between government and industry

Critical infrastructure and key asset protection concerns span all levels of government as well as the private sector. Protection over the long term is necessarily a shared responsibility that involves mustering resources and expertise nationwide. The *National Strategy for Homeland Security* recognizes the need to mobilize our entire society in a collective effort to defend our homeland. Accordingly, it places great emphasis on "the crucial role of state and local governments, private institutions, and the American people." This principle is central to our critical infrastructure and key asset protection effort.

Every disruption or attack is initially a local problem. Because of the immediate effects experienced by local communities, state and local governments, and private-sector infrastructure owners and operators invariably form the vanguard of response when terrorists strike. Consequently, public confidence depends heavily on how well the community implements protective measures and plans in advance of a crisis. Accordingly, the federal government will provide overall support, coordination, and focused leadership to foster an environment in which all stakeholders can better carry out their individual protection responsibilities.

4. Encourage market solutions whenever possible; compensate for market failure with focused government intervention

Protecting our Nation's critical infrastructures and key assets requires a broad spectrum of possible government actions, including: improving understanding and awareness of the current threat environment; providing threat indications and warnings; investing in research and development; transferring pilot technology; exploring various forms of financial incentives; and taking targeted regulatory action, where appropriate.

Through this *Strategy*, the federal government strives to encourage proactive, market-based protective solutions. Many of the critical infrastructure sectors are currently highly regulated, and additional regulatory directives or mandates should only be necessary in instances where market forces are insufficient to prompt the investments necessary to assure critical infrastructure and key asset protection. They may also be used when a uniform national standard or coordinated response is required to address a particularly challenging threat, especially in the context of cross-sector interdependencies.

In many cases, incentives can reinforce knowledge and experience within the private sector and state and local governments, including the development of new tools and innovative processes that are appropriate for their particular systems, operations, and security challenges. Incentives can also help to offset certain negative aspects of market dynamics, such as the natural tendency of market pressures to eliminate redundancies, and, hence, create single points of failure.

5. Facilitate meaningful information sharing

Information sharing underpins any true partnership and is necessary to mitigate the threat posed by a cunning, adaptive, and determined enemy. To

formulate comprehensive security plans and make informed security investment and action decisions, individuals and institutions alike require timely, accurate, and relevant information. Accordingly, we must adopt measures to identify and evaluate potential impediments or disincentives to security-related information sharing and formulate appropriate measures to overcome these barriers. We must also develop and facilitate reliable, secure, and efficient communications and information systems to support meaningful information sharing among various public- and private-sector entities.

6. Foster international security cooperation

Following the events of September 11, the United States moved quickly to engage friends and allies around the world in the war on terrorism. We also took prompt action with Canada and Mexico to initiate programs designed to improve the security of our shared borders and trans-border infrastructures. Further global engagement is needed to protect our critical infrastructures and key assets from terrorists. In a world characterized by complex interdependencies, international cooperation is a key component of our protective scheme.

7. Develop technologies and expertise to combat terrorist threats

The *National Strategy for Homeland Security* underscores the importance of science and technology as key elements of homeland security. Our efforts to secure critical infrastructures and key assets must fully leverage our technological advantages to make protection more effective,

more efficient, and less costly. Pooling our national resources and fostering collaboration between the public and private sectors will enable us to capitalize on emerging technologies and enhance our protection against the most lethal threats.

Similarly, through advances in modeling, simulation, and analysis we can improve our understanding of the complex, interdependent nature of the infrastructures and assets we must protect. Emergent capabilities in this area will facilitate protection planning, decision making, and resource allocation.

8. Safeguard privacy and constitutional freedoms

Our society is a tapestry of diverse races, ethnicities, cultures, religions, and political viewpoints. This pluralism and our ability as a society to accommodate diversity significantly contribute to America's strength. However, as the *National Strategy for Homeland Security* observes, our free society is also inherently vulnerable. Nevertheless, achieving security at the expense of the civil rights and liberties that form an integral part of our national character would hand a victory to terrorism.

Consequently, we must accept some level of terrorist risk as a persisting condition in our daily lives. The challenge is finding the path that enables us to mitigate risk and defend our country while preserving the freedoms and liberties that shape our way of life. In providing for our collective protection, we will respect privacy, the freedom of expression, the freedom of movement, the freedom from unlawful discrimination, and other cherished liberties that define us as a Nation.

ORGANIZING AND PARTNERING FOR CRITICAL INFRASTRUCTURE AND KEY ASSET PROTECTION

Implementing a comprehensive national critical infrastructure and key asset protection strategy requires clear and unifying organization, clarity of purpose, common understanding of roles and responsibilities, accountability, and a set of well-understood coordinating processes. A solid organizational scheme sets the stage for effective engagement and interaction between the public and private sectors. Without it, accomplishing the task of coordinating and integrating domestic protection policy, planning, resource management, performance measurement, and enabling initiatives across federal, state, and local governments, and the private sector would be impossible.

The work of providing a clearly defined and unifying organizational framework began with the publication of the President's *National Strategy for Homeland Security* and continues in this document. This chapter clarifies public- and private-sector roles and responsibilities for critical infrastructure and key asset protection. Ultimately, success lies in our ability to draw effectively and efficiently upon the unique core competencies and resources of each stakeholder. Given the range and complexity of required protection activities and the number of entities involved, clearly-defined authority, accountability, and coordinating processes will provide the foundation for a successful and sustainable national protection effort.

ORGANIZATION AND PARTNERING CHALLENGES

Overlapping federal, state, and local governance and the ownership structure of our critical infrastructures and key assets present significant protection challenges. The entities involved are diverse, and the level of understanding of protection roles and responsibilities differs accordingly. Furthermore, these organizations and individuals represent systems, operations, and institutional cultures that are complex and diverse. The range of protective activities that each must undertake is vast and varies from one enterprise to the next. Finally, overlapping protection authorities across federal, state, and local jurisdictions vary greatly. Success in implementing this *Strategy's* wide range of protection activities lies in establishing a unifying organizational framework that allows the development of

complementary, collaborative relationships and efficiently aligns our Nation's protection resources.

CLARIFYING ROLES AND RESPONSIBILITIES

In our federalist system of government, federal, state, and local governments and private industry have specific roles and perform certain functions that must be integrated to assure protection. Additionally, each critical infrastructure owner/operator possesses unique capabilities, expertise, and resources that, when integrated appropriately, can contribute to a comprehensive national protection effort.

Federal Government Responsibilities

The federal government has fundamental, clearly defined responsibilities under the Constitution. Providing for the common defense and promoting the general welfare of our country are among them. The federal government alone has the capability to use military, intelligence, and diplomatic assets to defend America's interests outside its borders. Closer to home, with support from state and local governments, the federal government has also traditionally led the effort to maintain the security of our borders. To prevent terrorists from entering the U.S., the federal government employs several tools unique to its arsenal, including: military, diplomatic, and intelligence-gathering activities; immigration and naturalization functions; and border agents, customs inspectors, and port and air terminal security.

The federal law enforcement apparatus consists of mechanisms that allow it to coordinate multi-jurisdictional approaches to security threats and incidents and the pursuit of perpetrators across state lines and overseas. Additionally, federal agencies conduct vital research activities, coordinate protection planning and incident management, and provide material and other types of support to state and local authorities. These capabilities serve as elements of deterrence, prevention, protection, and incident response.

Beyond such critical services and functions, the federal government has the capacity to organize, convene, and coordinate across governmental jurisdictions and the private sector. It therefore has the responsibility to develop coherent national policies, strategies, and programs. In the context of homeland security, the federal government will coordinate the complementary efforts and capabilities of government and private institutions to raise our level of protection over the long term for each of our critical infrastructures and key assets.

Every terrorist event has national impact. The federal government will therefore take the lead to insure that the three principal objectives defined in the *Introduction* of this *Strategy* are met. This leadership role involves:

- Taking stock of our most critical facilities, systems, and functions and monitoring their preparedness across sectors and governmental jurisdictions;

- Assuring that federal, state, local, and private entities work together to protect critical facilities, systems, and functions that face an imminent threat and/or or whose loss would have significant, national-level consequences;

- Providing and coordinating national threat assessments and warnings that are timely, actionable, and relevant to state, local, and private sector partners;

- Creating and implementing comprehensive, multi-tiered protection policies and programs;

- Exploring potential options for enablers and incentives to encourage public- and private sector entities to devise solutions to their unique protection impediments;

- Developing protection standards, guidelines, and protocols across sectors and jurisdictions;

- Facilitating the exchange of critical infrastructure and key asset protection best practices and vulnerability assessment methodologies;

- Conducting demonstration projects and pilot programs;

- Seeding the development and transfer of advanced technologies while taking advantage of private sector expertise and competencies;

- Promoting national-level critical infrastructure and key asset protection education and awareness; and

- Improving its ability to work with state and local responders and service providers through partnership.

As custodian of many of our Nation's key assets, such as some of our most treasured icons and monuments, and as the owner and operator of mission-critical facilities, the federal government also has significant, direct protection responsibilities. Accordingly, the federal government will take appropriate steps to:

- Identify its own critical facilities, systems, and functions;

- Identify the critical nodes upon which these assets depend;

- Assess associated vulnerabilities; and

- Implement appropriate steps to mitigate those vulnerabilities and protect the infrastructures and assets under its control.

Federal Lead Departments and Agencies

Each critical infrastructure sector has unique security challenges. The *National Strategy for Homeland Security* provides a sector-based organizational scheme for protecting America's critical infrastructures and key assets. (See *Federal Organization for Critical Infrastructure and Key Asset Protection*, p. 18.) This organizational scheme identifies the federal lead departments and agencies charged with coordinating

protection activities and cultivating long-term collaborative relationships with their sector counterparts.

In addition to securing federally-owned and -operated infrastructures and assets, the roles of the federal lead departments and agencies are to assist state and local governments and private-sector partners in their efforts to:

- Organize and conduct protection and continuity of operations planning, and elevate awareness and understanding of threats and vulnerabilities to critical facilities, systems, and functions;

- Identify and promote effective sector-specific, risk-management policies and protection practices and methodologies; and

- Expand voluntary, protection-related information sharing among private entities within sectors, as well as between government and private entities.

Each federal lead department or agency selects a "sector liaison," who represents industry's primary interface with the government. Industry's counterpart, the "sector coordinator," is designated by the federal lead department or agency to serve as a neutral party and facilitate sector coordination for a wide range of planning and activities to secure critical facilities and systems.

The federal government will expand on this model of public-private sector cooperation as a key component of our strategy for action. Accordingly, the federal lead departments and agencies of critical infrastructure sectors newly identified in the *National Strategy for Homeland Security* will take immediate steps to designate sector liaisons and coordinators and initiate protection activities. This will include identifying critical facilities, systems, and functions within their sectors and facilitating the development of sector protection plans.

Department of Homeland Security

The organizational model of federal lead departments and agencies provides a focused leadership structure for national-level protection coordination and planning. The newly created Department of Homeland Security (DHS) will significantly enhance the effectiveness of this model by providing overall cross-sector coordination. In this role, DHS will serve as the primary liaison and facilitator for cooperation among federal departments and agencies, state and local governments, and the private sector.

As the cross-sector coordinator, DHS will also be responsible for the detailed refinement and implementation of the core elements of this *Strategy*. This charter includes building and maintaining a complete, current,

and accurate assessment of national-level critical assets, systems, and functions, as well as assessing vulnerabilities and protective postures across the critical infrastructure sectors. DHS will use this information to assess threats, provide timely warnings to threatened infrastructures, and build "red team" capabilities to evaluate preparedness across sectors and government jurisdictions. Furthermore, DHS will collaborate with other federal departments and agencies, state and local governments, and the private sector to define and implement complementary structures and coordination processes for critical infrastructure and key asset protection. An effective starting point for this effort is the approach presently employed by federal lead departments and agencies and state and local governments to cooperate when responding to natural disasters.

In addition to cross-sector coordination, DHS will act as the federal lead department for several sectors, including government, emergency response, transportation, postal and shipping, and information and telecommunications.

To fulfill these responsibilities, DHS will:

Build partnerships with state and local governments and the private sector by designing and implementing its own processes to be open, inclusive, and results-oriented.

- Actively develop opportunities to build upon proven models;
- Identify and share the federal government's core competencies, capabilities, and selected resources to enhance the efforts of its partners; and
- Facilitate honest brokering and communication between organizations and sectors.

Office of Homeland Security

The Office of Homeland Security (OHS) will continue to act as the President's principal policy advisory staff and coordinating body for major interagency policy issues related to Homeland Security, including the critical infrastructure and key asset protection mission area. The functions of OHS will be to advise and assist the President in the coordination of the Executive Branch's efforts to detect, prepare for, prevent, protect against, respond to, and recover from terrorist attacks within the United States. OHS will work with the Office of Management and Budget (OMB) to integrate and endorse the President's critical infrastructure and key asset protection budget proposals. Under its existing authority, OHS will also work with OMB to certify that the budgets of other federal departments and agencies are sufficient to carry out their respective protection missions effectively.

FEDERAL GOVERNMENT ORGANIZATION TO
PROTECT CRITICAL INFRASTRUCTURE AND KEY ASSETS

President

Secretary of Homeland Security

Federal, state, local, and private sector coordination and integration
Comprehensive national infrastructure protection plan
Mapping threats to vulnerabilities and issuing warnings

Sector	Lead Agency
Agriculture	Department of Agriculture
Food:	
Meat and poultry	Department of Agriculture
All other food products	Department of Health & Human Services
Water	Environmental Protection Agency
Public Health	Department of Health & Human Services
Emergency Services	Department of Homeland Security
Government:	
Continuity of government	Department of Homeland Security
Continuity of operations	All departments and agencies
Defense Industrial Base	Department of Defense
Information and Telecommunications	Department of Homeland Security
Energy	Department of Energy
Transportation	Department of Homeland Security*
Banking and Finance	Department of the Treasury
Chemical Industry and Hazardous Materials	Environmental Protection Agency
Postal and Shipping	Department of Homeland Security
National Monuments and Icons	Department of the Interior

* Under the *Homeland Security Act of 2002*, the Transportation Security Administration, responsible for securing our Nation's transportation systems, will become part of the Department of Homeland Security. The new Department will coordinate closely with the Department of Transportation, which will remain responsible for transportation safety.

Other Federal Departments and Agencies

Besides the designated federal lead departments and agencies, the federal government will integrate the unique expertise and skill sets of numerous other departments and agencies to enhance the physical protection dimension of homeland security. For example, the National Institute of Science and Technology's (NIST's) National Standards and Measurements Laboratory will play a significant role in standards-setting for the critical infrastructure and key asset protection mission. Recent examples of this role are reflected in the language of the *USA Patriot Act of 2001, Enhanced Border Security and Visa Reform Act of 2002,* and *National Construction Safety Team Act.*

Overall sector initiatives will often comprise international components, require the development of coordinated relationships with foreign governments or agencies, and entail information sharing with foreign governments. Accordingly, the Department of State (DoS) will support the development and implementation of protection initiatives by laying the groundwork for bilateral and multilateral infrastructure protective agreements with our international friends and allies. Through its unique responsibility to lead U.S. foreign policy and support the programs and efforts of other federal departments and agencies, DoS will play a key role in advancing our critical infrastructure and key asset priorities.

State and Local Government Responsibilities

The 50 states, 4 territories, and 87,000 local jurisdictions that comprise this Nation have an important and unique role to play in the protection of our critical infrastructures and key assets. All U.S. states and territories have established homeland security liaison offices to manage their counter-terrorism and infrastructure protection efforts. In addition, the states have law enforcement agencies, National Guard units, and other critical services that can be employed to protect their communities.

Like the federal government, states should identify and secure the critical infrastructures and key assets under their control. With the support of federal lead departments and agencies, states should also promote the coordination of protective and emergency response activities and resource support among local jurisdictions and between regional partners. States should further facilitate coordinated planning and preparedness by applying unified criteria for determining criticality, prioritizing protection investments, and exercising preparedness within their jurisdictions. They should also act as conduits for requests for federal assistance when the threat at hand exceeds the capabilities of state and local jurisdictions and the private entities within them. States should also facilitate the exchange of relevant security information and threat alerts down to the local level.

Many states have well-organized relationships with one another through various organizations, such as the National Emergency Managers Association and the National Governors Association, as well as through mutual support agreements. Coordinating with one another, they can capitalize on their mutual capabilities through regional approaches to protection. As proven during September 11 response efforts, mutual aid agreements and other such successful cooperative processes for crisis management demonstrate the competence of various jurisdictions and organizations to plan and work together.

At the onset, every disruption or attack is a local problem. Regardless of who owns and operates the affected infrastructure, each requires an immediate response by local authorities and communities who must support the initial burden of action before the incident escalates to a national event.

Local governments represent the front lines of protection and the face of public services to the American people. Their core competencies must include knowledge of their communities, residents, landscapes, and existing critical services for maintaining public health, safety, and order. Communities look to local leadership to assure safety, economic opportunities, and quality of life. Public confidence, therefore, starts locally and is dependent upon how well communities plan and are able to protect their citizens, respond to emergencies, and establish order from chaos. When local authorities succeed in preventing or mitigating loss of life or property, or, as in New York City on September 11, respond to disaster with clarity of purpose and effectiveness, they affirm their capabilities and bolster public confidence. For this reason, local communities play critical roles in preparing their citizens for emergencies and engaging their public and private leadership in the development of coordinated local and regional plans to assure the protection of residents and businesses.

State and local governments look to the federal government for support and resources when national requirements exceed their capabilities to fulfill them. Protecting critical infrastructures and key assets will require a particularly close and well-organized partnership among all levels of government. DHS, in particular, will provide a single point of coordination for state and local governments for homeland security issues. Other federal lead departments and agencies and federal law enforcement organizations will provide

support as needed and appropriate for specific critical infrastructure and key asset protection issues.

Private-Sector Responsibilities

The lion's share of our critical infrastructures and key assets are owned and operated by the private sector. Customarily, private companies prudently engage in risk management planning. They also invest in security as a necessary component of their business operations and to assure customer confidence. In the present threat environment, the private sector remains the first line of defense for its own facilities. Consequently, private-sector owners and operators should reassess and adjust their planning, assurance, and investment programs to accommodate the increased risk presented by deliberate acts of terrorism. Since the events of September 11, enterprises nationwide have increased their investments in security to meet the demands of the new threat environment.

For most enterprises, the level of security investment they undertake reflects implicit risk-versus-consequence tradeoffs, which are determined based on: (1) what is known about the risk environment, and (2) what is economically justifiable and sustainable in a competitive marketplace or in an environment of limited resources. Given the dynamic nature of the terrorist threat and the severity of the potential consequences associated with many potential attack scenarios, the private sector will look to the government to help better inform its crucial security investment decisions. Similarly, the private sector will require assistance when the threat exceeds an enterprise's capability to protect itself beyond a reasonable level of security investment. The federal government will collaborate with public- and private-sector entities to assure the protection of nationally critical infrastructures and assets, provide timely warnings and help assure the protection of infrastructures that are specifically threatened, and promote an environment in which the private sector can better carry out its specific protection responsibilities.

The availability of both timely, credible information and relevant expertise, complemented by inclusive access to affordable tools and best practices, encourages the private sector to make prudent investments earlier and at all levels of the risk management spectrum. By developing mutually beneficial relationships and coordinating protection efforts, public-private partnership can significantly enhance our Nation's ability to protect its critical infrastructures and key assets.

Working with DHS and other federal lead departments and agencies, sector coordinators will play a crucial role in enabling this collaboration. Sector coordinators will also work with the government to identify, promote, and share industry-specific best practices. To fulfill their protection agendas, sector coordinators will rely on DHS and other federal lead departments and agencies to provide consistent guidance and criteria for sector-specific protection planning and investment as well as for relevant, actionable, and timely indications and warnings. The private sector may also require incentives to stimulate investment. Accordingly, sector liaisons and sector coordinators will work with their counterparts to explore potential catalysts and reduce the barriers to public-private sector cooperation.

In addition to formal government support, private industry can take many steps to improve its own security posture across the board. Many industries have developed alliances to sustain reliability and assure public confidence in their national-level infrastructures. Because the public's perception of a sector's overall performance can affect the shareholder values of its individual members, many institutions cooperate within a framework for sharing operational and security-related best practices. Sectors whose constituent enterprises are highly interconnected have also developed mutual aid agreements to prevent the disruption of one member's systems from cascading to others across the sector. Reliability activities of the energy sector, specifically the electricity industry, are an example of an effective critical infrastructure partnership.

Even before the September 11 attacks, several critical infrastructure industries had already established Information Sharing and Analysis Centers (ISACs) to formalize information exchange among their members and improve the management of operational risks from physical and cyber disruption. Moreover, many sector organizations, working with their federal counterparts, have also developed plans to contribute to the national protection effort. Federal support of sector ISACs and protection planning must now expand to include the newly designated critical infrastructure sectors.

Partnership will provide the foundation for developing and implementing coordinated protection strategies. True partnerships require continuous interaction and, above all, trust. Currently, however, there are barriers impeding the public and private sectors from achieving a relationship of this level. Many current attitudes and institutional relationships, processes, and structures are products of a bygone era. Safeguarding our critical infrastructures and key assets from terrorism in today's fluid marketplace and threat environment requires a new, more cooperative set of institutional relationships and attitudes. The need for partnering is clear.

CROSS-SECTOR SECURITY PRIORITIES

This chapter addresses the overarching, cross-sector initiatives that represent our national-level priorities for critical infrastructure and key asset protection. The focus is on cross-sector protection issues and activities that require immediate attention, encourage cooperation, and increase the cost-effectiveness of security investments. The protection initiatives outlined herein also support the three underlying objectives of this *Strategy*: (1) identifying and assuring the protection of our most nationally critical infrastructures and assets; (2) providing timely warning and assuring the protection of infrastructures and assets that face a specific, imminent threat; and (3) fostering an environment in which all stakeholders can better protect the infrastructures and assets under their control.

We have entered a fluid threat environment in which security must be viewed as an integral component of core practices and standard operations—not a box to be checked before addressing other issues. As the threat of terrorism persists and evolves, we must be able to adapt our security planning and protection efforts to remain effective and sustainable over the long term. The activities that follow in this *Strategy* represent the first steps in this national journey.

The cross-sector security initiatives addressed in this chapter fall into the following categories:

- Planning and Resource Allocation

- Information Sharing and Indications and Warnings

- Personnel Surety, Building Human Capital, and Awareness

- Technology and Research & Development

- Modeling, Simulation, and Analysis

Each section describes a cross-sector protection issue as well as the impediments to protection associated with that issue. It then identifies specific actions that will be taken to address those challenges and remove barriers hindering the implementation of needed protection activities.

PLANNING AND RESOURCE ALLOCATION

Effective and efficient risk assessment, protection planning, and resource allocation go hand in hand. They depend upon the ability of federal, state, and local governments, the private sector, and our international partners to work together to articulate and attain their individual and shared goals, requirements, and priorities.

State and local governments currently face unprecedented demands for their limited resources. Declines in revenues mean that states and local communities often lack the resources to undertake a full spectrum of prudent critical infrastructure protection measures. Because of these resource limitations, federal, state, and local authorities must collaborate more efficiently to assess, plan, and allocate their limited resources.

Industry is likewise coping with the consequences of dynamic threats and difficult economic environments. In some cases, certain critical-sector enterprises are concentrating their resources solely on remaining in business. To instill greater stability in the security investment process, it will be necessary for private-sector organizations to closely coordinate critical infrastructure protection plans and programs to ensure that federal and state governments, in particular, understand and recognize their future spending landscape.

Risk assessment and management must also be closely integrated and coordinated. Industries and institutions are in need of a common vocabulary and standards to guide their protection efforts. Close cooperation among all levels of government and the private sector both nationally and internationally is essential to developing a shared vernacular and vision for the future.

Planning and Resource Allocation Challenges

Heavy demands on state and local resources, uncertainties created by a lack of coordination, and dynamics of the terrorist threat underlie many of the challenges of the domestic protection environment. Since the September 11 attacks, state and local governments have been called upon to provide increased security for their critical infrastructures and key assets, border areas, airports, and seaports. Unanticipated revenue declines have affected most states and challenged their abilities to meet the requirements of operating under balanced budgets. Hence, they cannot increase expenditures to account for additional protective measures without making corresponding reductions in spending for other programs and services.

We often rely on state and local jurisdictions to protect key national assets (e.g., bridges, tunnels, nuclear power plants, dams, and airports). Conversely, state and local governments request federal resources at times to ensure the protection of their own critical infrastructures and key assets. Under uncertain and sustained elevated threat conditions, determining how best to allocate the scarce resources of the various jurisdictions responsibly and appropriately will require unprecedented levels of cooperation across all levels of government.

Another resource allocation challenge relates to the mechanisms through which states must apply for federal assistance. Current policies and procedures sometimes create inefficiencies in the federal grant decision-making process. Because they must seek funding from various sources according to different guidelines, state and local government officials often view complying with grant requirements and review processes as leading to duplications of effort. Rectifying the lack of streamlined mechanisms for providing federal funding to state and local governments will require a thorough cross-agency review.

Engaging U.S. states and territories in a collaborative framework for infrastructure protection is another important planning challenge. State and local law enforcement agencies and emergency responders are the first line of defense against deliberate acts of violence. In fact, state and local jurisdictions continue to bear a large share of post-September 11 security expenditures nationwide. Their concerns and constraints must be recognized and factored into our national protective scheme.

A key challenge in prioritizing efforts to enhance infrastructure protection is the difficulty in estimating the economic damage that could result from a terrorist attack. Such damage includes both the immediate effects of a strike (e.g., losses to plant and equipment) as well as any subsequent long-term economic losses. The cascading effects often overshadow short-term repercussions over time, yet they are extremely difficult to estimate. Relatively short-term disruptions to critical operations can produce significant downstream economic effects (e.g., price changes, lost contracts, lost financing, and losses in insurability). Predicting the extent of such effects accurately requires acute sensitivity to the myriad of interdependencies present in modern industrial and financial markets.

In the risk management process, certain aspects of criticality determination may also produce inadvertent consequences. Designating certain facilities as "critical" in conjunction with domestic protection efforts may result in their becoming more difficult and expensive to insure and operate. The federal government must work in concert with other key stakeholders to explore options for incentives to compensate for the costs engendered by the current threat environment.

Aligning disparate assessment methodologies presents another challenge. Presently, multiple methodologies from various departments and agencies are currently being used to assess vulnerabilities. In many cases, they are neither consistent, nor comparable, thereby complicating protection planning and resource allocation across the board.

Many critical infrastructures also cross international borders, raising unique protection challenges. We must, therefore, work closely with our friends and allies around the world to develop plans to secure the interconnected infrastructures that make up the international marketplace.

Planning and Resource Allocation Initiatives

It is incumbent in the planning and resource allocation process that federal, state, and local governments and private-sector stakeholders work together to:

- Define clearly their critical infrastructure and key asset protection objectives;

- Develop a business case for action to justify increased security investments;

- Establish security baselines, standards, and guidelines; and

- Identify potential incentives for security-related activities where they do not naturally exist in the marketplace.

To enable such actions, we will:

Create collaborative mechanisms for public- and private-sector critical infrastructure and key asset protection planning

DHS and other federal lead departments and agencies will enable and encourage the development of clearly defined collaborative mechanisms through which the public and private sectors can cooperate in national-level protection planning and performance measurement. The federal government will also work in conjunction with other stakeholders to assess critical infrastructure and asset vulnerabilities, share information, develop protection strategies and plans to eliminate or mitigate these vulnerabilities, and develop restoration and recovery plans for implementation in the aftermath of an attack. DHS will assess these sector plans for clarity, comprehensiveness, consistency, and resource prioritization.

DHS will also assimilate the individual sector plans into a comprehensive national plan for critical infrastructure and key asset protection to inform the federal government's annual process of planning, programming, and budgeting for national-level protection activities.

Identify key protection priorities and develop appropriate supporting mechanisms for these priorities

DHS, in collaboration with other key stakeholders, will develop a uniform methodology for identifying facilities, systems, and functions with national-level criticality to help establish federal, state, and local government and the private-sector protection priorities. Using this methodology, DHS will build a comprehensive database to catalog these critical facilities, systems, and functions. DHS will also maintain a comprehensive, up-to-date assessment of vulnerabilities and preparedness across critical sectors. This effort will help guide near-term protective actions and provide a basis for long-term leadership focus and informed resource investment.

DHS will furthermore establish a multi-year approach for critical infrastructure and key asset protection to instill predictability and structure in the planning process.

Foster increased sharing of risk-management expertise between the public and private sectors

Many different risk assessment methodologies are in use based on a wide variety of requirements and standards. Government and industry could each benefit greatly from the extensive experience of the other. DHS will coordinate the sharing of lessons learned and best practices to build a common

domestic protection assessment framework that is adaptable to different user environments.

Identify options for incentives for private organizations that proactively implement enhanced security measures

Consulting with the private sector, DHS will work with the Department of Commerce (DoC) and the Department of the Treasury to identify appropriate options for developing cost-effective incentives to compensate stakeholders for enhanced security investments.

This could include rewarding early adopters of new policies or providing various incentives for incorporating security enhancements into critical sector products and services.

Coordinate and consolidate federal and state protection plans

DHS will work with other federal departments and agencies to consolidate federal protection plans to clarify roles, responsibilities, and expectations. DHS will also work with the states to coordinate protection-planning efforts and provide them with a clear roadmap for action. Additionally, the Homeland Security Advisory System will be coordinated with state-level critical infrastructure and key asset protection plans.

Establish a taskforce to review legal impediments to reconstitution and recovery following an attack against a critical infrastructure or key asset

DHS, in concert with the Department of Justice (DoJ), will convene representatives from federal, state, and local governments, and the private sector to scrutinize regulatory and licensing procedures that could impede reconstitution of critical infrastructure service in emergencies and identify options for resolving them.

Reconstitution requirements for critical infrastructures may necessitate the waiving of established licensing and regulatory procedures during

emergencies. Procedures for establishing these "post incident rule sets" need to be predetermined as part of part of a collaborative public-private partnership.

Develop an integrated critical infrastructure and key asset geospatial database

To enable effective critical infrastructure and key asset protection planning, analysis, and decision support. we must develop an integrated critical infrastructure and key asset geospatial database for access and specific use by federal, state, and local government officials, and the private sector.

A geospatial assurance partnership of appropriate government departments and agencies is needed to serve as the imagery/geospatial data broker, integrator, and coordinator for this database. DHS and other federal departments and agencies will continue current efforts to acquire data for priority population centers, domestic critical infrastructure sectors, and transborder infrastructures in cooperation with the private sector. This database will provide a common frame of reference for senior public- and private-sector decision makers and operational planners in support of vulnerability analysis, domestic preparedness. and incident management.

Conduct critical infrastructure protection planning with our international partners

In the aftermath of the September 11 attacks. we developed comprehensive bilateral critical infrastructure protection framework agreements and began a series of protection initiatives with our Canadian and Mexican neighbors. DHS, in concert with DoS and other federal departments and agencies will work to expand this security collaboration to include other key international partners. The overall objective of this effort will be to determine our transborder infrastructure vulnerabilities and implement measures to eliminate or mitigate these vulnerabilities.

INFORMATION SHARING AND INDICATIONS AND WARNINGS

To meet the challenges associated with the terrorist threat, public- and private-sector critical infrastructure and key asset protection stakeholders must have the ability to work together seamlessly. The federal government—particularly the intelligence and law enforcement communities—has a significant role in providing, coordinating, and ensuring that threat information is understood across all levels of government. Likewise, state and local law enforcement and private-sector security entities are also valuable sources of localized threat information. Additionally, they possess a much better understanding of the vulnerabilities impacting their facilities, systems, and functions than does the federal government. Development of accepted and efficient processes and systems for communication and exchange of crucial security-related information is critical to bridging existing gaps and building a foundation for cooperation.

The difficulties and roadblocks routinely faced by those attempting to share security information serve as major impediments to progress in the critical infrastructure and key asset protection mission area. An extraordinary level of cooperation and perseverance will be required to change the status quo. Federal, state, and local governments and the private sector must make every effort to promote effective information sharing and embrace efforts to establish timely, effective, and useful paths of communication between those who need it most. Information is a crucial tool in fighting terrorism, and getting the right information to the right party at the right time is a top priority.

Adequate protection of our critical infrastructures and key assets requires:

* Improved collection of threat information;

* Comprehensive and relevant threat assessment and analysis;

* Robust indications and warning processes and systems; and

* Improved coordination of information sharing activities.

Accurate, timely information is a fundamental element of our national critical infrastructure and key asset protection effort. It underpins all components of our protection strategy and enables preventive action, warning, preparation, and crisis response. Presently, major impediments exist to accomplishing effective

information sharing among all levels of the public and private sectors. Overcoming these obstacles entails:

* Identifying what is to be accomplished by exchanging security-related information;

* Defining the type of information that must be shared to accomplish that purpose;

* Determining how and when to share and safeguard critical security information most properly;

* Deciding who the appropriate recipients of such information will be;

* Assigning responsibility for analyzing information and determining the threat implications; and

* Assigning responsibility for appropriate action once that information has been analyzed and the threat implications are clear.

Information Sharing and Indications and Warnings Challenges

The overall management of information sharing activities among government agencies and between the public and private sectors has lacked proper coordination and facilitation. As a result, the existing national mechanisms for collecting threat information, conducting risk analyses, and disseminating warnings have been inadequate for the domestic protection mission.

State and local governments and private sector officials have indicated that the threat information they receive from the federal government is often vague, duplicative,

and—in some cases—conflicting. They argue that they seldom receive indications and warnings that are specific, accurate, and timely enough to support difficult resource allocation decisions. Conversely, when relevant, timely information is shared, they point out that it often fails to reach the appropriate parties because of security clearance requirements.

Additionally, the current security clearance process is redundant and costly, with lengthy delays. In one example, current regulations require certain state and local law enforcement officials to be screened twice, once by state and local authorities and again by the federal government. We must streamline this process to make it more responsive to our protection needs.

In fact, protecting the Nation's critical infrastructures and key assets may not necessarily require such clearance for all stakeholders. If intelligence sources and methods are omitted, many intelligence reports may be declassified. Time-efficient procedures are needed to declassify relevant intelligence or extract information from classified sources and disseminate that information to the appropriate recipients. These concerns are complicated by the ineffective means by which sensitive information is transferred, as well as the mechanisms currently in place to ensure that required information is disseminated appropriately. Currently, there is no central, coordinating mechanism to assess the impact of sensitive information and ensure that it gets to all the parties with a need to know. Adding to this problem is the lack of technical communications systems to enable the secure transmittal of classified threat information to the owners and operators of concern.

The above issues pose a significant challenge and stand in the way of the partnership our Nation needs to assure the protection of its critical infrastructures and key assets. Underlying these issues is an inherent lack of trust among key stakeholders that we must overcome. Without all pieces of the information puzzle, we operate from a major disadvantage in the fight against terrorism.

Information Sharing and Indications and Warnings Initiatives

The enactment of the *Homeland Security Act of 2002*, the *Act*, represents substantial progress in removing the legal obstacles that stand in the way of information sharing between the public and private sectors. The *Act* provides that critical infrastructure information voluntarily submitted to DHS, when accompanied by an express statement of the expectation that it will be protected, will be exempt from disclosure under the *Freedom of Information Act* and state "Sunshine" laws. Further, if such information is submitted in good faith.

it may not be directly used in civil litigation without the consent of the person submitting it.

The *Act* also provides for the establishment of governmental procedures for receiving, handling, and storing voluntarily submitted critical infrastructure information and for protecting the confidentiality of such information. It also provides for the development of mechanisms that, while preserving confidentiality, also permit the sharing of such information within the federal government and with state and local governments. The *Act* authorizes the federal government to provide advisories, alerts, and warnings to relevant businesses, targeted sectors, other governmental actors, and the general public regarding potential threats to critical infrastructure. The *Act* also stipulates that the federal government must protect the source of any voluntarily submitted information forming the basis of a warning as well as any proprietary or other information that is not properly in the public domain.

Finally, the *Act* enables private-sector actors to enter into voluntary agreements to promote critical infrastructure security, including appropriate forms of information sharing, without incurring the risk of antitrust liability. Under this new legal regime, DHS will be able to give proper assurances to private-sector owners and operators of critical infrastructure that the sensitive or proprietary information that they furnish will be protected. These assurances will encourage the private sector—which is uniquely positioned to provide information about the vulnerabilities of the infrastructure it owns and operates—to share that vital information with the government. At the same time, government will ensure that such action does not diminish competition in the market place.

Creating a more effective and efficient information-sharing regime to enable our core protective missions will require further government leadership and intense collaboration between public- and private-sector stakeholders. Specific initiatives include efforts to:

Define protection-related information sharing requirements and establish effective, efficient information sharing processes

One of the first steps we must take is to precisely define information sharing requirements as they pertain to the critical infrastructure and key asset protection mission. These requirements should focus on the sharing of real-time threat, vulnerability, and incident data; best practices; security guidelines; risk assessments; and operational procedures. DHS, in conjunction with DoJ, DoS, and other federal lead departments and agencies, will lead efforts to

establish this two-way requirements framework in collaboration with other key stakeholders, including international partners. Once requirements are determined, processes must be established to ensure that the appropriate users can access needed information in a timely manner.

Implement the statutory authorities and powers of the Homeland Security Act of 2002 to protect security and proprietary information regarded as sensitive by the private sector

To facilitate meaningful information exchange between the public and private sectors, we will implement the provisions of the *Act* rapidly to encourage the private sector to share sensitive security-related information and incident data. Accordingly, within the framework established by the *Act*, DHS will work with DoJ, Congress, other federal lead departments and agencies, and state lawmakers to:

- Implement appropriate protections for the private sector to share vulnerability assessments, incident reports, and other security data with government; and

- Explore appropriate mechanisms to share and exchange security-related information with our international partners.

Promote the development and operation of critical sector Information Sharing Analysis Centers

Sector-focused ISACs provide a model for public-private sector information sharing, particularly in the area of indications and warnings. Numerous critical infrastructure sectors use this structure to communicate potential risks, threats, vulnerabilities, and incident data among their constituent memberships.

ISACs generally have mechanisms in place that allow them to share many categories of relevant, sensitive information in a timely manner. Although the ISACs have proven to be a successful information sharing model thus far, their capabilities could be greatly improved, particularly with respect to developing advanced analytical capabilities. DHS and other federal lead departments and agencies will provide increased support to sector efforts to exchange security-related information via the ISACs. Additionally, DHS will work with industry to establish processes and mechanisms to help incorporate state and local government participation into the ISAC process.

Improve processes for domestic threat data collection, analysis, and dissemination to state and local government and private industry

Our intelligence community has longstanding processes for collection, analysis, and dissemination of information on threats to our national security interests. We must establish similar collection and assessment processes are needed to integrate information from all sources in the context of domestic critical infrastructure and key asset protection.

Additional processes must be put in place to ensure that state and local law enforcement and infrastructure and key asset owners and operators have full and timely access to needed information, including assessments of terrorist organization tactics, techniques, and procedures; assessments of terrorist capabilities and motivations; lessons learned from terrorist operations in other countries; and the comprehensive mapping of these products to sector vulnerabilities.

DHS, in collaboration with the intelligence community and the DoJ, will develop comprehensive threat collection, assessment, and dissemination processes that integrate intelligence and law enforcement capabilities relevant to the domestic protection mission. They will also develop processes to ensure that the results of this fusion of relevant intelligence and law enforcement data are disseminated to the appropriate stakeholders in a timely manner. This includes exploring ways to expedite the conduct of necessary background checks and issuance of security clearances to those with a need to know.

Support the development of interoperable secure communications systems for state and local governments and designated private sector entities

DHS will enlist the assistance of experts from NIST, the Department of Defense (DoD), and other appropriate organizations to develop technical systems for the sharing of sensitive information and then help state and local governments acquire access to them.

Complete implementation of the Homeland Security Advisory System

The Homeland Security Advisory System was implemented in early 2002. DHS will continue to work with other federal departments and agencies, state and local governments, and the private sector to interpret, harmonize, and identify appropriate actions that correspond to the various threat levels included in this system as they relate to their particular assets and operations.

PERSONNEL SURETY, BUILDING HUMAN CAPITAL, AND AWARENESS

Domestic security starts in our communities, in our own institutions, and in our businesses. Those who have access to and operate our critical infrastructures and key assets are crucial to our national protective scheme. The key issues impacting personnel surety, building human capital, and awareness encompass four main areas:

- Developing safeguards to prevent an insider or a disaffected or co-opted employee from conducting sabotage activities or facilitating terrorist access to a critical facility or system;

- Recruiting and training more skilled operations and security personnel to protect our critical infrastructures and key assets;

- Assuring that these workers are secure while doing their jobs; and

- Implementing communication and awareness programs to help businesses and communities take action to protect their respective assets and manage risk constructively.

Personnel Surety

The September 11 attacks demonstrated that terrorist organizations possess the capability to conduct long-term clandestine operations, with individual members blending into daily life in the United States. The "insider threat" is becoming an increasingly serious concern for critical infrastructure and key asset protection across all sectors. An "insider" is defined as an employee or anyone else who has routine access to critical facilities and systems. This group also includes contractors, temporary help, and outsourcers. Insiders, because of their access and positions of trust, can intentionally or unwittingly become terrorist surrogates by disclosing information relevant to critical nodes, vulnerabilities, operating characteristics, or security measures. They can also provide terrorists with direct access to and mobility within critical facilities and systems, such as operations centers and control rooms.

Building Human Capital

Related to personnel surety is the fundamental need to ensure that trustworthy, reliable, and trained personnel are available to protect critical infrastructures and key assets from terrorist attack. Private sector owners and operators depend on skilled employees to accomplish the protection mission. Security personnel and first responders, in particular, require adequate training, equipment, and other support to carry out their responsibilities effectively and with some degree of assurance that their personal security will not be in jeopardy while accomplishing their mission.

Awareness

A state of sustained preparedness requires widespread consciousness among members of the public—especially among those in government and the private sector most directly affected—of the scope and nature of the threat we face and the precautions we must take to meet the threat. The federal government, working with the private sector, has been engaged for several years in a systematic program to develop protection awareness among key business leaders in the critical sectors. This effort, which has increased significantly since September 11, has been especially productive. Additionally, the scope of the attacks themselves and the extensive publicity they engendered (e.g., congressional hearings and media coverage) have significantly raised public consciousness of the terrorist threat. This level of awareness must be sustained over the long term for our national protective effort to be truly successful.

Personnel Surety, Building Human Capital, and Awareness Challenges

Time-efficient, thorough, and periodic background screening of candidate employees, visitors, permanent and temporary staff, and contractors for sensitive positions is an important tool for protecting against the "insider threat." Unfortunately, in-depth personnel screening and background checks are often beyond the capabilities of private sector and non-federal government entities. Private employers also lack access to personnel reliability data—often in the possession of the federal government—that could help determine whether employees, contractors, and visitors should be employed at or allowed access to sensitive facilities. Part-time, temporary, and seasonal workers also challenge effective background screening processes because of the high level of employee turnover. Other challenges include concern for constitutional freedoms, costs associated with screening processes, and a lack of verifiable documentation and other sources of information.

Aside from personnel surety, shortages of skilled personnel in various professions—ranging from security technicians to emergency first responders—also impede critical infrastructure and key asset protection. Similarly, although private security officers are identified as an important source of protection for critical facilities, few formal standardized qualifications, training, or certification requirements exist for these positions across the critical sectors. Given the dynamic nature of the terrorist threat, there is an urgent need for ongoing training of security personnel to sustain skill levels and to remain up-to-date on evolving terrorist weapons and tactics.

Protection of employees from the terrorist threat or exposure to the potential aftereffects of an attack is an important concern for critical infrastructure and key asset owners and operators. They are also potential disincentives for their employees, security personnel, and first responders. Future attacks could result in biological, chemical, or radiological contaminants at an incident site that, without proper precautions, could endanger emergency workers, their families (by cross-contamination), and others in the exposed areas.

Despite the events of September 11, awareness of the implications of terrorist threats to critical infrastructures among members of industry in general remains relatively low. As time passes and focus on the events of that day recedes, the awareness and interest of the general public also recedes. As a result, security-related activities could lack the consistent focus required to assure protection, thus leaving us exposed once more.

Personnel Surety, Building Human Capital, and Awareness Initiatives

To overcome the challenges described above, we will:

Coordinate the development of national standards for personnel surety

DHS, in concert with DoJ, will convene an advisory task force to perform a comprehensive review of critical infrastructure sector personnel surety programs. The task force—to be comprised of federal agencies and departments, state and local governments, and private sector representatives—will develop advice on the creation of national standards and capabilities for background checks, screening, criminal investigations, and positive identification of key personnel employed in critical service sectors.

Harmonizing personnel surety policies and programs among critical infrastructure sectors will help create uniform standards and address concerns articulated by businesses regarding the adequacy of background checks for occupants of critical job categories. In developing national standards for personnel surety, however, we must find the balance that enables us to mitigate risk and defend our country while preserving individual freedoms and liberties.

Develop a certification program for background-screening companies

To complement private-sector employer efforts, DHS, in concert with DoJ, will develop a certification program for background-screening companies to ensure a base-line level of competence and reduce obstacles to timely and accurate verification of employee backgrounds and investigative histories.

In addition, DHS will initiate a study to identify options for creating or enabling access to databases to accredit candidates for critical positions and other potential hires, contract workers, and key service supplier personnel. Federal databases, such as those operated by the Immigration and Naturalization Service and various intelligence and law enforcement agencies, could be used to seed this process. As we undertake this effort, we must take the precautions necessary to protect individual constitutional freedoms.

Explore establishment of a certification regime or model security training program for private security officers

To maximize the effectiveness of the Nation's corps of private security personnel, DHS will work with law enforcement and federal security officials to initiate a dialogue with state and local counterparts,

private-sector infrastructure owners and operators, and private security firms concerning the creation of a training and certification regime for private security officers. One possible model is the program for security training provided by the federal law enforcement academies.

Identify requirements and develop appropriate programs to protect critical personnel

DHS will work with state and local government and industry representatives to identify requirements and develop appropriate programs to protect critical personnel who may become terrorist targets because of their roles in protection activities.

Security and first responder personnel must be assured of their own personal safety while engaging in their protection and response missions. These personnel may need to be equipped with the protective devices and clothing necessary to shield them from toxic or biological contamination and impede the transmission of potentially dangerous agents to others. In this regard, personal protective equipment must be developed with the needs of law enforcement and other first responders uppermost in mind across the critical infrastructure sectors. Programs must be implemented to ensure that security personnel and first responders receive protection training and education necessary for them to carry out their responsibilities.

Facilitate the sharing of public- and private-sector protection expertise

DHS, in concert with other federal lead departments and agencies, will develop a program to facilitate the sharing of protection expertise between the public and private sectors.

Training and exercises that test protection plans and personnel capabilities are critical to assessing required improvements in preparedness and sharing best practices. Accordingly, DHS will also develop and incorporate realistic hands-on and virtual exercises into its critical infrastructure and key asset protection education and training programs with the objective of exploring common protection issues and solutions. With proper design, these exercises can serve important outreach, training, coordination, and evaluation purposes across the public and private sectors.

Develop and implement a national awareness program for critical infrastructure and key asset protection

DHS, in concert with other key stakeholders, will identify and assess the requirements for a comprehensive, national awareness program that will support sustainability of preparedness programs, security investment, and protection activities, as well as the public's understanding of the terrorist threat environment.

Building awareness means creating a national appreciation for how security must be fundamentally incorporated into our daily lives and business operations. Our national awareness program should focus on the specific needs of the critical infrastructure industries to support informed private-sector decisions and enable the planning of relevant and effective protection strategies and resource allocation.

It must also be sufficiently comprehensive in scope to maintain the public's understanding and appreciation of the threat environment as it evolves and foster confidence in the strategies and approaches being taken to address it.

TECHNOLOGY AND
RESEARCH & DEVELOPMENT

The terrorist threat challenges us to marshal our nation's advantages in the sciences and technology. Protecting our Nation's critical infrastructures and key assets against this threat will require a systematic, national effort to fully harness our research and development (R&D) capabilities. Doing so will enable us to meet many of our immediate needs for protective standards and solutions. It will also help lay the long-term foundation for developing the advanced tools and technologies that will enable more comprehensive and cost-effective protection solutions in the future, particularly regarding the most catastrophic threats we may have to confront.

Organizing this national effort will require persistence, careful planning, and coordination. Our national research enterprise is vast and complex. Private companies, universities, research institutions, and government laboratories of all sizes are conducting pure and applied research to develop the advanced materials, products, and services that will contribute to assuring the protection of critical infrastructures and key assets.

To best realize these advances, however, we must be able to identify needs—standards, tools, and processes—that span multiple sectors as a critical first step. Accomplishing this will enable us to establish research priorities and concentrate efforts and assign responsibilities in these areas while avoiding unnecessary duplication that can draw valuable capacity away from other needed research. It will also provide researchers, engineers, and infrastructure owners and operators with a minimum threshold of capabilities to guide product development efforts and provide end users a metric to gauge the sufficiency of the technological solutions they adopt.

Technology and Research & Development Challenges

The number and diversity of stakeholders present impediments to coordinating technological R&D activities for critical infrastructure and key asset protection. Organizations at each level of government and across the critical infrastructure sectors all have individual R&D priorities and interests intended to identify solutions to the particular problems they consider most important. One major challenge at the outset is to define the points of commonality among these disparate needs and efforts to determine where coordinated R&D activities will yield value across the broadest range of interests.

At the national level, the general lack of focus on long-term research, development, testing, and engineering for critical infrastructure and key asset protection is a significant shortfall in our current domestic protection posture. A need exists for a process to coordinate, with broad sector input, the creation and adoption of national research priorities, and support to cross-sector R&D activities.

In addition, our domestic protection requirements create a demand for new tools to contribute to security at the operational level. In this regard, we must work to improve our capability to conduct a wide range of tests on potential contaminants (e.g., biological, chemical, and radiological) that can be used to threaten our food and agriculture, water, mass transit, and other sectors. Similarly, we must expand our monitoring and surveillance capabilities to improve our ability to detect the presence of weapons of mass destruction and their components.

An especially great need exists for standards to support interoperable communications. The current lack of capability in this area consistently ranks as one of the most critical shortcomings in our protection and emergency response posture across the Nation. At present, federal, state, and local law enforcement personnel and fire, medical, and emergency management personnel use incompatible communications systems, introducing difficulties and barriers in information exchange and security operations. This lack of common standards in

communications equipment can seriously impede close collaboration among security personnel, first responders, state emergency management personnel, and federal officials prior to, during, and in the aftermath of a terrorist incident. Responses to terrorist incidents can be further complicated if differences in communications connectivity themselves become a target for terrorist exploitation.

The lack of reliable tools to authenticate the identities of personnel with direct access to our most critical facilities and systems also impedes security across sectors. A similar situation exists with respect to identification of law enforcement, fire, and emergency response personnel working in protection and incident response roles.

Finally, harmonizing the oftentimes conflicting need to enhance security while simultaneously maintaining reasonably open channels of commerce requires both new tools and processes that challenge technology. For example, critical dams, particularly those on navigable waterways, present difficult security challenges. The locks on such dams must remain available for the flow of commerce, yet waterborne threats must be abated. Other sectors such as air transportation, rail and maritime shipping, and site security at major commercial and government buildings, national landmarks, and the like present similar needs for effective, non-invasive monitoring and sensor capabilities.

Technology and Research & Development Initiatives

To respond to these challenges, government and industry must work together to develop standards in security technology for both physical and information infrastructures. Such standards would enable key stakeholders to collaborate more effectively to develop the products essential to enhancing the security of infrastructures and managing the interdependencies among them.

Accordingly, we will:

Coordinate public- and private-sector security research and development activities

DHS will coordinate with other appropriate federal agencies to support security technology research and development, including specialized pilot programs and projects. This effort will include exploration of mechanisms to migrate technologies developed by the DoD and other government agencies to the private sector for use in infrastructure protection. Activities in this area will include appropriate collaboration with our international partners to expand our research base and capitalize on technological solutions being developed by our friends and allies.

Coordinate interoperability standards to ensure compatibility of communications systems

We will act to establish and disseminate interoperability standards to ensure compatibility of communications systems used by federal, state, and local authorities. The Federal Communications Commission (FCC), will lead this effort, working in concert with DHS, other federal lead departments and agencies such as DOC's National Telecommunications and Information Administration, other standard-setting bodies such as NIST, affected user groups, and equipment manufacturers. Establishment of standards will enable secure and assured interoperable communications among all levels of homeland security entities. Standardized communication systems will enhance protection and incident response, as well as promote efficient planning and training at all levels.

Explore methods to authenticate and verify personnel identity

We must provide better means of identifying people in order to increase the security of our critical facilities, systems, and functions. We must create a uniform means of identifying law enforcement and security personnel and individuals with access to critical facilities and systems.

Technologies to be examined for this authentication scheme include biometric identifiers, magnetic strips, microprocessor-enabled "SMART" cards, and other systems. Such tools would enable quick authentication of identities in the protection and emergency response domains. The enhanced "scene control" entailed would facilitate investigations at the sites of terrorism incidents, and create an investigative baseline for comparing different analytical data.

Improve technical surveillance, monitoring and detection capabilities

We must improve our technical surveillance, detection (including non-invasive inspection methods), and monitoring systems for perimeter, entry area, and key node vigilance. We must also develop more robust detection systems for use by security personnel across our critical infrastructure sectors.

DHS, in collaboration with other public- and private-sector stakeholders, will develop a research agenda to explore technical solutions to surveillance and detection deficiencies in critical sectors, to include capabilities to detect chemical, biological, and radiological (CBR) residues.

MODELING, SIMULATION, AND ANALYSIS

Modeling, simulation, and analysis activities help to prioritize critical infrastructures and key assets protection activities and investments. This *Strategy* has discussed the challenges and uncertainties presented by critical nodes and single-points-of-failure within infrastructures, as well as increasing interdependencies that exist among the various infrastructure sectors both nationally and internationally. These interdependencies and key nodes are often difficult to identify and resolve, as are the cascading and cross-sector effects associated with their disruption. Properly employed, modeling, simulation, and analysis can provide valuable, predictive insights into potential consequences that could result from these dependencies and interdependencies in various threat scenarios.

Modeling, simulation, and analysis can also facilitate protection planning and decision support by enabling the mapping of complex interrelationships among the elements that make up the risk environment. For example, modeling traffic patterns through a particular junction, such as rail or air traffic through a key railhead or air terminal, allows analysis of the various possible outcomes of an attack on that node at various points in time. Such information would be helpful in drawing attention to likely cascading consequences that otherwise might have gone unconsidered.

Using models and simulations, responsible authorities can evaluate the risks associated with particular vulnerabilities more accurately and subsequently make more informed protection decisions. Modeling and simulation can also be used as a real-time decision support tool to help mitigate the effects of an attack or avert a secondary attack altogether.

Private-sector infrastructure and asset owners and operators possess considerable experience in preparing for and responding to a wide variety of naturally occurring events like floods, earthquakes, and hurricanes. Their expertise in planning and response stems from long histories of contending with the challenges associated with these naturally occurring phenomena. In contrast, the pervasive threat of terrorist strikes against our critical infrastructures and key assets is relatively new. Hence, no similar long-term data exist that track the patterns of such deliberate incidents; nor is there evidence as to which safeguards would be most effective, making the need to develop reliable, predictive surrogate data even more important.

Modeling, Simulation, and Analysis Challenges

Historically, we have relied on modeling, simulation, and analysis capabilities to enable decision support and planning activities related to national defense and intelligence missions. We must now find ways to employ them to develop creative approaches and enable complex decision support, risk management, and resource investment activities to combat terrorism at home.

Modeling, simulation, and analysis would provide significant value to many sectors across government and the economy. Demands for such studies will likely be great; and, as in the case of R&D planning, we will have to establish priorities among the projects to be undertaken, giving emphasis to those studies that are likely to yield common benefits and address the most stressing threats and vulnerabilities.

Improving our modeling and simulation resources must also include an effort to enhance data collection and standardization. Currently, much data relevant to national-level protection activities may not exist, be accessible, or reside in a standard format. Data collection processes, systems, and standards will have to be created and adopted to provide common representations of data across models and simulations.

Furthermore, enhancing our national modeling, simulation, and analysis capabilities will require a unified effort across the public and private sectors to yield the results needed in the most efficient and cost-effective manner possible. Through effective partnering across the federal interagency community, state and local government, national laboratories, academia, and commercial enterprises, we can enlist tremendous talents and resources to drive this capability forward. Cross-sector collaboration is also essential to establishing standard methodologies and consistent analytical frameworks for interpreting research results, especially when modeling infrastructure interdependencies.

Most industry officials have a fairly complete understanding of their own operations and associated vulnerabilities. However, many of these enterprises require assistance to identify their dependencies on other sectors and the degree of risk to which they are exposed as a function of those interdependencies. The potential impact of such interdependencies hit home for the banking and financial services sector on September 11, when the collapse of the World Trade Center towers interrupted telecommunications services in lower Manhattan. The disruption brought electronic financial transactions to a halt, with long-term economic impacts still being felt more than a year later.

In most cases, modeling and simulation capabilities are not well integrated into existing infrastructure protection planning activities. Achieving this integration will be critical to the task of translating modeling and simulation research data into effective guides for sector-focused protection planning, decision support, and resource allocation.

Modeling, Simulation, and Analysis Initiatives

Modeling, simulation, and analysis initiatives that we will pursue across the critical infrastructure sectors include efforts to:

Integrate modeling, simulation, and analysis into national infrastructure and asset protection planning and decision support activities

DHS will establish an advisory panel consisting of representatives from the public and private sectors, national laboratories, academia, and commercial research organizations to explore alternatives to integrate modeling and simulation activities into domestic protection planning.

The panel will be charged to review modeling, simulation, and analysis and advise DHS on ways to focus on-going and planned research activities on national priorities. Early in the process, emphasis will be given to developing and disseminating standards and methods for modeling sector interdependencies. Such standards will be based on a clear definition of assets or services deemed to be critical and will be tasked for development through nationally coordinated planning activities overseen by DHS.

Develop economic models of near- and long-term effects of terrorist attacks

The economic significance of terrorist attacks is not always clear, with short-term effects often only partially predictive of longer-term realities. Models of the temporal and cross-sector scope of economic damage caused by physical infrastructure attacks would assist policymakers and emergency management specialists in understanding and mitigating worst case effects.

Develop critical node/chokepoint and interdependency analysis capabilities

Fundamental to the core objective of modeling interdependencies and mapping the consequences of particular terrorist events, we will also undertake research to develop metrics for gauging the adequacy of infrastructure subsystems and key nodes compared to level of threat and effect. This includes comparing the robustness of different infrastructures at points where key centers or critical nodes are in close proximity to one another and can have cascading effects if attacked. Clearly identifying and addressing interdependencies among critical infrastructures in both a national and international context is high on our list of protection priorities.

Model interdependencies among sectors with respect to conflicts between sector alert and warning procedures and actions

Modeling alert responses and possible counter-productive effects of alert system designs will enhance flexibility and minimize duplication of effort. The intent of raising the Homeland Security Alert status is to trigger actions to protect infrastructures and make it more difficult for terrorists to act. These actions, however, may have disruptive consequences that may themselves interact in ways that could create additional vulnerabilities.

Conduct integrated risk modeling of cyber and physical threats, vulnerabilities, and consequences

Risk assessments help to identify and determine ways to manage risk to best allocate resources. These assessments include threat analysis to provide a baseline and frame of reference for risk management and investment decisions. This analysis, coupled with vulnerability assessments to determine the effectiveness of security systems and tools to provide consequence analysis, will provide information on critical assets and nodes. Such studies would comprise models of security incidents involving various types of both cyber and physical attacks. Analysis will focus on the complex interactions between physical and cyber systems to determine the full range of potential consequences and to ensure the applicability of findings across infrastructures in both a domestic and international context.

Develop models to improve information integration

The integration of threat and vulnerability information between sectors needs to be modeled, as does information sharing between the federal government and critical infrastructures, to identify points of inefficiency and information loss.

SECURING CRITICAL INFRASTRUCTURES

Our society and modern way of life depend on a complex system of critical infrastructures. The *National Strategy for Homeland Security* has identified 13 critical sectors. As we learn more about threats, means of attack, and the various criteria that make targets lucrative for terrorists, this list will evolve. The critical infrastructure sectors consist of agriculture and food, water, public health, emergency services, government,[1] the defense industrial base, information and telecommunications,[2] energy, transportation, banking and finance, chemicals and hazardous materials, and postal and shipping.[3] Common issues of concern to these sectors are described in the *Cross-Sector Security Priorities* chapter of this strategy.

For each critical sector, this chapter discusses:

- Unique characteristics of the infrastructure sector itself and the industry that supports it;

- Current efforts that are underway to protect sector-specific goods and service delivery and associated critical assets, systems, and functions;

- Unique protection challenges; and

- Priority protection action areas for the sector to address in a collaborative fashion.

Consistent with the principles of this *Strategy*, any initiatives involving significant federal resources will be prioritized across the critical sectors, taking into account the risks and consequences of potential threats and the proper sharing of protection responsibilities among the various stakeholders.

---

1 The primary focus of this *Strategy* is the physical protection of critical infrastructures and key assets. Each lead federal department and agency has developed a continuity of operations plan (COOP) to ensure the continuity of government (COG) for its sector. As these plans are classified, COG will not be discussed in this document.

2 The protective strategy for information technology and network assets for specific sectors is discussed in detail in the *National Strategy to Secure Cyberspace*. Accordingly, the protection of the Information Technology component of the Information and Telecommunications sector is not discussed in this document.

3 The protection of National Monuments and Icons is addressed in Chapter VII, "Protecting Key Assets."

AGRICULTURE AND FOOD

From farm to table, our Nation's agriculture and food systems are among the most efficient and productive in the world. These industries are a source of essential commodities in the U.S., and they account for close to one-fifth of the Gross Domestic Product. A significant percentage of that figure also contributes to our export economy, as the U.S. exports approximately one quarter of its farm and ranch products.

The Agriculture and Food Sectors include:

- The supply chains for feed, animals, and animal products;

- Crop production and the supply chains of seed, fertilizer, and other necessary related materials; and

- The post-harvesting components of the food supply chain, from processing, production, and packaging through storage and distribution to retail sales, institutional food services, and restaurant or home consumption.

Changes in the ways that food is produced, distributed, and consumed present new challenges for ensuring its safety and security. More of our food is grown abroad, many foods are transported long distances, and we eat away from home more frequently. Public confidence in the safety of agricultural and food-processing and packaging systems represents a key part of sustaining the economic viability of these sectors. America's reputation as a reliable supplier of safe, high quality foodstuffs is likewise essential to maintaining the

confidence of foreign customers who are important to the national economy as a whole.

The United States has a strong, well functioning food-safety system to protect the public against unintentional contamination of food products. Besides the agriculture and food industries' measures to ensure food safety, the overall mechanism includes extensive analyses of critical control points in the food supply chain and federal, state, and local inspections of food processing and storage facilities, as well as food service establishments. Sector enterprises are currently in the process of assessing physical security practices and procedures in place at their facilities, particularly processing plants.

Agriculture and Food Sector Challenges

The fundamental need for food, as well as great public sensitivity to food safety makes assuring the security of food production and processing a high priority.

Our food and agriculture industries have been developed over several decades and are unique with respect to their structures and processes. The greatest threats to the food and agricultural systems are disease and contamination, in which case, sector decentralization represents a challenge to assuring their protection. Government and industry have worked together in the past to deal with isolated instances of deliberate food tampering. The effectiveness of the food safety system with regard to preventing, detecting, and mitigating

the effects of unintentional or isolated contaminations offers a foundation to build upon for countering deliberate acts to corrupt the food supply.

Because of the food system's many points of entry, detection is a critical tool for securing the agriculture and food sectors. There is an urgent need to improve and validate analytical methods for detecting bioterrorist agents in food products, as well as a need for enhanced laboratory capabilities and capacities. The existing system of federal, state, and local public health and agriculture laboratories was established to detect the presence of traditional human pathogens that occasionally and unintentionally contaminate foods. Although this system continues to serve an important role in safeguarding public health from these traditional agents, its capabilities must be enhanced to enable protection from a wide spectrum of nontraditional agents. This enhanced system must also be capable of eliminating the occurrence of false positives for threat agents in food and agricultural products in addition to inconsistencies in detecting them when they are present.

Additionally, we must expand our system of laboratories to accommodate the requirements that could result from a bioterrorist attack on the food supply. We must also increase the number of qualified personnel (veterinarians and lab technicians) and laboratories with the ability to diagnose and treat animal disease outbreaks and crop contamination. Moreover, many state budgets for such inspection, detection, and training protocols will need to be revisited to provide for such initiatives.

Moving and processing crops and animals require transporting them over long distances. During transport, these resources spend time in storage areas and facilities where they may come in contact with other products. Accordingly, the agriculture and food sectors depend on transportation system owners and operators, particularly regarding trucks and containers, to meet the safety and security standards necessary to protect food products in transit. We must improve mechanisms designed to track the movement of animals and commodities in transit and enable officials to pinpoint where an outbreak or contamination originates.

Rapid acquisition and use of threat information could help to prevent an attack from spreading beyond individual facilities or local communities to become a regional or national problem. Unfortunately, serious institutional barriers and disincentives for sharing such information exist within the sectors and their structures. For instance, there are significant, direct economic

disincentives associated with reporting problems or suspected contamination in food processing.

Meanwhile, the agriculture and food markets are highly competitive, and many parts of the food system operate within slim profit margins. As a result, some companies may be more likely to hold onto information related to incidents involving suspected contamination in order to prevent the potential financial consequences of what might be a false alarm.

Protecting the public from an outbreak or contamination incident requires timely reporting of information for prompt decision-making and action. In the current environment, when crops or animals must be culled or preventively killed to deal with disease or contamination, the fear of a negative public response and attendant economic implications to the sector may impede the needed levels of response in the agriculture and food sectors.

Deliberate contaminations by terrorists aim to harm people or animals to the greatest extent possible. Another principal objective is to create panic and inflict economic damage. Because of the influence the media has on how the public responds to incidents, clear and accurate communication of information to news outlets is essential. Official spokespersons at state, regional, and national levels should be pre-assigned. Although food regulators routinely communicate with industry on food-safety issues, planning for public communications in the event of a deliberate contamination should also be a priority, as should defining stakeholder responsibilities within those plans.

Agriculture and Food Sector Initiatives

Information derived from assessment of sector food-safety processes and procedures can provide a foundation for developing an agriculture and food sector critical infrastructure protection system. For example, two major efforts to establish procedures for accidental outbreaks of animal disease have already been completed.[1] While plans for these studies were drafted with accidental introductions of disease or contamination in mind, their findings and recommendations may also apply to intentional acts. Another example of ongoing activities in this area is the implementation of recommendations from the 1999 Animal and Plan Health Inspection report, *Safeguarding American Plant Resources*. Further study and collaborative policy development are required to determine whether and how the food safety system could be extended to deal with food security issues.

Additional agriculture and food sector protection initiatives include efforts to:

Evaluate overall sector security and identify and address vulnerabilities

DHS and the Departments of Agriculture (USDA) and Health and Human Services (HHS), working in collaboration with state and local governments and industry, will undertake a broad risk assessment of the agriculture and food sectors to evaluate overall security and identify and address existing vulnerabilities.

Enhance detection and testing capabilities across the agricultural and food networks

DHS, USDA, and HHS, in collaboration with state and local governments and industry, will work to increase detection and testing capacity. Exploring mechanisms to improve detection capabilities, ranging from technology development to increasing the number of veterinary, epidemiology, and technical specialists at the state level, will facilitate earlier detection and response. Enhancing trace-back systems and increasing detection capabilities at borders and ports of origin will also significantly increase protection. Identifying, creating, and certifying additional laboratory capacity across the country would likewise increase the speed of analysis and response.

Assess transportation-related security risks

DHS, USDA, HHS, and the Department of Transportation (DoT) will work with representatives from the agriculture and food industries to assess security risks in food and commodity transport and develop appropriate solutions. The scope of the issues requires a thorough risk assessment integrating transportation security measures into ongoing and newly initiated countermeasures undertaken by the food industry. Additional considerations include standardizing the methods by which the agriculture and food industries report truck hijackings and cargo thefts, and then disseminating these reports within the food industry.

Identify potential infrastructure protection incentives; identify and address existing disincentives

DHS working with USDA and HHS will explore options for developing incentives or reducing disincentives to encourage the prompt reporting of problems.

Develop emergency response strategies

DHS, USDA, and HHS, working with sector counterparts, will develop a strategy to coordinate risk communications and other emergency response activities.

---

1   These efforts are reported in *The Animal Health Safeguarding Review: Results and Recommendations*, October 2001, by the National Association of State Departments of Agriculture Research Foundation, and *The U.S. National Animal Health Emergency Management System, 2001 Annual Report*.

WATER

The Nation's water sector is critical from both a public health and an economic standpoint. The water sector consists of two basic, yet vital, components: fresh water supply and wastewater collection and treatment. Sector infrastructures are diverse, complex, and distributed, ranging from systems that serve a few customers to those that serve millions. On the supply side, the primary focus of critical infrastructure protection efforts is the Nation's 170,000 public water systems. These utilities depend on reservoirs, dams, wells, and aquifers, as well as treatment facilities, pumping stations, aqueducts, and transmission pipelines. The wastewater industry's emphasis is on the 19,500 municipal sanitary sewer systems, including an estimated 800,000 miles of sewer lines. Wastewater utilities collect and treat sewage and process water from domestic, commercial, and industrial sources. The wastewater sector also includes storm water systems that collect and sometimes treat storm water runoff.

The water sector has taken great strides to protect its critical facilities and systems. For instance, government and industry have developed vulnerability assessment methodologies for both drinking water and wastewater facilities and trained thousands of utility operators to conduct them. In response to the *Public Health Security and Bioterrorism Preparedness and Response Act of 2002*, the Environmental Protection Agency (EPA) has developed baseline threat information to use in conjunction with vulnerability assessments. Furthermore, to defray some of the cost of those studies, the EPA has provided assistance to drinking water systems to enable them to undertake vulnerability assessments and develop emergency response plans.

To improve the flow of information among water-sector organizations, the industry has begun development of its sector-ISAC. The Water ISAC will provide a secure forum for gathering, analyzing, and sharing security-related information. Additionally, several federal agencies are working together to improve the warehousing of information regarding contamination threats, such as the release of biological, chemical, and radiological substances into the water supply, and how to respond to their presence in drinking water. With respect to identifying new technologies, the EPA has an existing program that develops testing protocols and verifies the performance of innovative technologies. It has also initiated a new program to verify monitoring technologies that may be useful in detecting or avoiding biological or chemical threats.

Water Sector Challenges

The basic human need for water and the concern for maintaining a safe water supply are driving factors for water infrastructure protection. Public perception regarding the safety of the Nation's water supply is also significant, as is the safety of people who reside or work near water facilities. In order to set priorities among the wide range of protective measures that should be taken, the water sector is focusing on the types of infrastructure attacks that could result in significant human casualties and property damage or widespread economic consequences. In general, there are four areas of primary concentration:

- Physical damage or destruction of critical assets, including intentional release of toxic chemicals;

- Actual or threatened contamination of the water supply;

- Cyber attack on information management systems or other electronic systems; and

- Interruption of services from another infrastructure.

To address these potential threats, the sector requires additional focused threat information in order to direct

investments toward enhancement of corresponding protective measures. The water sector also requires increased monitoring and analytic capabilities to enhance detection of biological, chemical, or radiological contaminants that could be intentionally introduced into the water supply. Some enterprises are already in the process of developing advanced monitoring and sampling technologies, but additional resources from the water sector will likely be needed. Environmental monitoring techniques and technologies and appropriate laboratory capabilities require enhancement to provide adequate and timely analysis of water samples to ensure early warning capabilities and assess the effectiveness of clean-up activities should an incident occur. Specific innovations needed include new broad-spectrum analytical methods, monitoring strategies, sampling protocols, and training.

Approaches to emergency response and the handling of security incidents at water facilities vary according to state and local policies and procedures. With regard to the public reaction associated with contamination or perceived contamination, it is essential that local, state, and federal departments and agencies coordinate their protection and response efforts. Maintaining the public's confidence regarding information provided and the timeliness of the message is critical. Suspected events concerning water systems to date have elicited strong responses that involved taking systems out of service until their integrity could be verified, announcing the incident to the public, and issuing "boil water" orders.

The operations of the water sector depend extensively on other sectors. The heaviest dependence is on the energy sector. For example, running pumps to move water and wastewater and operating drinking water and wastewater treatment plants require large amounts of electricity. To a lesser extent, the water sector also depends on the transportation system for supplies of water treatment chemicals, on natural gas pipelines for the energy used in some operational activities, and on the telecommunications sector. Water and wastewater systems are increasingly automated and controlled from remote locations for efficiency.

Water Sector Initiatives

Water infrastructure protection initiatives are guided both by the challenges that the water sector faces and by recent legislation.[1] Additional protection initiatives include efforts to:

Identify high-priority vulnerabilities and improve site security

EPA, in concert with DHS, state and local governments, and other water sector leaders, will work to identify processes and technologies to better secure key points of storage and distribution, such as dams, pumping stations, chemical storage facilities, and treatment plants. EPA and DHS will also continue to provide tools, training, technical assistance, and limited financial assistance for research on vulnerability-assessment methodologies and risk-management strategies.

Improve sector monitoring and analytic capabilities

EPA will continue to work with sector representatives and other federal agencies to improve information on contaminants of concern and to develop appropriate monitoring and analytical technologies and capabilities.

Improve sector-wide information exchange and coordinate contingency planning

DHS and EPA will continue to work with the sector coordinator and the water ISAC to coordinate timely information on threats, incidents, and other topics of special interest to the water sector. DHS and EPA will also work with the sector and the states to standardize and coordinate emergency response efforts and communications protocols.

Work with other sectors to manage unique risks resulting from interdependencies

DHS and EPA will convene cross-sector working groups to develop models for integrating priorities and emergency response plans in the context of interdependencies between the water sector and other critical infrastructures.

---

1 On June 12, 2002, President Bush signed the *Public Health Security and Bioterrorism Preparedness and Response Act of 2002 (Bioterrorism Act)* into law. The *Bioterrorism Act* requires many drinking water systems to conduct vulnerability assessments, certify and submit copies of their assessments to EPA, and prepare or revise their emergency response plans.

PUBLIC HEALTH

The public health sector is vast and diverse. It consists of state and local health departments, hospitals, health clinics, mental health facilities, nursing homes, blood-supply facilities, laboratories, mortuaries, and pharmaceutical stockpiles.

Hospitals, clinics, and public health systems play a critical role in mitigating and recovering from the effects of natural disasters or deliberate attacks on the homeland. Physical damage to these facilities or disruption of their operations could prevent a full, effective response and exacerbate the outcome of an emergency situation. Even if a hospital or public health facility were not the direct target of a terrorist strike, it could be significantly impacted by secondary contamination involving chemical, radiological, or biological agents.

In addition to established medical networks, the U.S. depends on several highly specialized laboratory facilities and assets, especially those related to disease control and vaccine development and storage, such as the HHS Centers for Disease Control and Prevention, the National Institutes of Health, and the National Strategic Stockpile.

Public Health Sector Challenges

Public health workers are accustomed to placing themselves in harm's way during an emergency. They may be unlikely, however, to view themselves as potential targets of terrorist acts.

Most hospitals and clinics are freely accessible facilities that provide the public with an array of vital services. This free access, however, also makes it difficult to identify potential threats or prevent malicious entry into these facilities. This fact, combined with a lack of means and standards to recognize and detect potentially contaminated individuals, can have an important impact on facility security and emergency operations.

Another significant challenge is the variation in structural and systems design within our hospitals and clinics. On one hand, so-called "immune buildings" have built-in structural design elements that help prevent contamination and the spread of infectious agents to the greatest extent possible. Such features include controlled airflow systems, isolation rooms, and special surfaces that eliminate infectious agents on contact. At the other extreme are buildings with relatively little built-in environmental protection. Protection of this category of facility presents the greatest challenge.

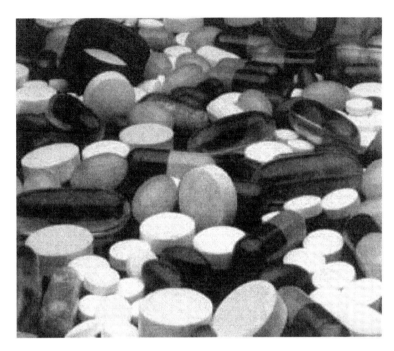

During an epidemic, infectious individuals who continue to operate in the community at large may pose a significant public health risk. The sector needs to develop comprehensive protocols governing the isolation of infectious individuals during a crisis.

Additional public health sector challenges relate to the maintenance, protection, and distribution of stockpiles of critical emergency resources. Currently, other than the National Strategic Stockpile, there are limited resources for rotating and replenishing supplies of critical materials and medicines. Supply chain management for medical materials also requires greater attention to ensure secure and efficient functioning during an emergency. Potential solutions to these problems are impacted by complex legal and tax issues. Currently, the federal government has only limited regulatory authority to request information from companies concerning their available inventory of medical supplies and their capacity to produce them. Since pharmaceutical companies are taxed on their product inventories, they try to avoid stockpiling finished goods and meet demand through "just-in-time" manufacturing.

Sector-specific legal and regulatory issues also tend to impede the effective protection of assets and services. The *Emergency Medical Treatment and Active Labor Act* requires hospitals to treat patients requiring emergency care regardless of their insurance status. Disaster

situations involving mass casualties tax the resources of critical facilities in terms of manpower, medical supplies, and space. As patients are stabilized, it is often necessary to transfer them to other hospitals to free up critical resources for newly arriving casualties. With respect to disaster victims without insurance, however, once treatment is no longer an emergency, hospitals are not bound to treat them. As a result, many second-tier, noncritical hospitals will not or cannot accept uninsured patients, thereby requiring the critical hospital by default to continue nonemergency treatment. Additionally, privacy rules mandated in the *Health Insurance Portability and Accountability Act* should be reviewed to determine whether they could prevent the sharing of critical data in the event of an epidemic.

Existing security challenges have focused the public health sector on assessing its ability to deliver critical services during a crisis. Many hospitals, however, are faced with operating at limited profit margins and, therefore, have difficulty making appropriate security investments.

Finally, specialized medical and pharmaceutical laboratories merit special attention—particularly those handling highly toxic or infectious agents. These facilities are mission-critical with respect to identifying hazardous agents should an attack or outbreak occur. These facilities also enable the containment, neutralization, and disposal of such hazardous materials. Overcoming the protection challenges associated with securing these specialized assets is a top priority.

Public Health Sector Initiatives

Public health sector protection initiatives include efforts to:

Designate trusted communicators

HHS will work with state and local public health officials to identify, appoint, train, and prepare recognized subject matter experts to speak on behalf of the public health sector in times of crisis. These appointees would act as important envoys of homeland security information to communicate consistent, accurate information, as well as to inform, instruct, and reassure the American public. Additionally, HHS leaders will be prepared to play substantial roles at the national level in communicating with the public regarding risks associated with bioterrorism or other public health emergencies.

Review mission critical operations, establish protection priorities, and ensure adequate security and redundancy for critical laboratory facilities and services

HHS will work with hospitals and clinics in the public health sector to review their mission-critical systems and operations and help them create detailed plans to focus security investments and increase their protection. In partnership with state health departments, HHS and DHS will identify and prioritize national-level critical hospitals and medical centers, as well as their most important component facilities, systems, and services.

HHS and DHS will work with the health care sector to ensure that key laboratory facilities are protected and have adequate redundancy with respect to critical capabilities and data systems.

Enhance surveillance and communication capabilities

HHS will assist public health sector officials to identify requirements for robust surveillance systems and coordinate links between public health monitoring facilities and healthcare delivery systems.

Develop criteria to isolate infectious individuals and establish triage protocols

HHS will work with state and local health officials to develop isolation and quarantine standards to improve the protection of the unaffected population during a public health crisis. HHS will also work with state and local health officials during consequence management planning to set priorities for the deployment of vaccination and prophylaxis resources in of the event of a terrorist incident involving biological or chemical weapons.

Enhance protection of emergency stockpiles of medical supplies and domestic and international pharmaceutical manufacturing facilities

HHS and DHS will work with the health care sector to enable the protection of stockpiles of medical supplies and other critical materials, distribution systems, and the critical systems of medical institutions, including basic surveillance capabilities necessary for tracking the spread of diseases and toxic agents. Additionally, HHS will identify providers of critical resources and ensure a ready stockpile of vital medicines for use in an emergency.

Explore options for incentives to increase security spending

In partnership with state health departments, HHS will examine legal and regulatory impediments that could prevent critical health facilities from providing critical services during a crisis. HHS will also explore possible incentives to encourage increased investment in the physical security of facilities in the public health sector. The current federally sponsored investment program to improve critical hospital capabilities within local communities provides an appropriate point of departure for this effort.

EMERGENCY SERVICES

The emergency services infrastructure consists of fire, rescue, emergency medical service (EMS), and law enforcement organizations that are employed to save lives and property in the event of an accident, natural disaster, or terrorist incident.

Emergency Services Sector Challenges

Lessons learned from the September 11 attacks indicate that the most pressing problems to be addressed in this sector include: inadequate information sharing between different organizations—particularly between law enforcement and other first responders; telecommunications problems, such as a lack of redundant systems; and the challenge of enhancing force protection through such measures as stronger crime scene control and enhanced security to mitigate secondary attacks.

Terrorists pose a major challenge to our national emergency response network. Although the existing infrastructure is sufficient for dealing with routine accidents and regional disasters, the September 11 attacks revealed shortfalls in its specific capabilities to respond to large-scale terrorist incidents and other catastrophic disasters requiring extensive cooperation among local, state, and federal emergency response organizations. Most pressing among these shortfalls has been the inability of multiple first-responder units, such as police and fire departments, to coordinate their efforts—even when they originate from the same jurisdiction.

Major emergencies require cooperation by multiple public agencies and local communities. Systems supporting emergency response personnel, however, have been specifically developed and implemented with respect to the unique needs of each agency. Such specification complicates interoperability, thereby hindering the ability of various first responder organizations to communicate and coordinate resources during crisis situations.

Robust communications systems are essential for personnel safety and the effective employment of human resources during a crisis or an emergency. Failure of communications systems during a crisis impedes the speed of response and puts the lives of responders at risk. Another important issue is the extent to which emergency response communications depend on key physical nodes, such as a central dispatcher, firehouse, or 911-call center.

Unlike most critical infrastructures, which are closely tied to physical facilities, the emergency services sector consists of highly mobile teams of specialized

personnel and equipment. Another challenge for the emergency services sector, therefore, is assuring the protection of first responders and critical resources during emergency response operations. Future terrorist incidents could present unseen hazards at incident sites, including the risk of exposure to CBR agents. Moreover, past experience indicates that emergency services response infrastructure and personnel can also be the targets of deliberate direct or secondary attacks, a bad scenario that could be made worse by communication difficulties and responding units that are ill-prepared for such a likelihood.

Preparedness exercises serve to provide experience and feedback on preparation for response and emergency management activities. Various state and local governments and federal agencies have hosted local or regional exercises. The approaches used vary widely—a fact that could impede the effectiveness of multi-jurisdictional response efforts.

Faced with the threat of a major terrorist attack, no single jurisdiction has the ability to maintain or assemble all of the resources necessary to provide an effective response. Mutual aid agreements facilitate the flow of public safety personnel, equipment, and other vital resources across jurisdictional boundaries to enable local communities to help each other during emergencies and disasters.

Emergency Services Sector Initiatives

Emergency services sector protection and response initiatives include efforts to:

Adopt interoperable communications systems

DHS and DoJ will work with state and local governments and other appropriate entities to study and resolve important communications interoperability issues. This problem is already widely recognized and accepted as a valid concern at the state and local government level. The common, overriding need to assure effective communications during an emergency can be used as a catalyst to drive individual agencies toward a solution.

Develop redundant communications networks

DHS will work with state and local officials to develop redundant emergency response networks to improve communications availability and reliability, especially during a major disruption.

Implement measures to protect our national emergency response infrastructure

DHS will inventory and analyze the vulnerability of our national emergency response infrastructure, including critical personnel, facilities, systems, and functions. DHS will work with states, localities, and other entities to develop plans to assure the safety of personnel during response efforts, as well as the protection of our emergency response critical infrastructure.

Coordinate national preparedness exercises

DHS will work with state and local governments to develop a coordinated national emergency response exercise program. Coordinated preparedness exercises would promote consistency in protection planning and response protocols and capabilities at the regional and national levels, as well as provide a forum for sharing lessons learned and best practices.

Enhance and strengthen mutual aid agreements among local jurisdictions

DHS will work with officials from local communities to strengthen existing mutual aid agreements and develop new ones in regions across the U.S. where needed. Furthermore, it will promote discussion regarding the adoption of common standards and terminology for equipment and training.

DEFENSE INDUSTRIAL BASE

Our nation's defense and military strength rely primarily on the DoD and the private sector defense industry that supports it. Without the important contributions of the private sector, DoD cannot effectively execute its core defense missions, including mobilization and deployment of our nation's military forces abroad. Conversely, private industry and the public at large rely on the federal government to provide for the common defense of our Nation and protect our interests both domestically and abroad.

Success in the war on terrorism depends on the ability of the United States military to mount swift, calculated offensive and defensive operations. Ensuring that our military is well trained and properly equipped is critical to maintaining that capability. Private industry manufactures and provides the majority of the equipment, materials, services, and weaponry used by our armed forces. For several decades, DoD has worked to identify its own critical assets and systems. It has also begun to address its dependency on the defense industrial base, and is now taking the concerns of private industry into consideration in its critical infrastructure protection assessment efforts.

Market competition, consolidations, globalization, and attrition have reduced or eliminated redundant sources of products and services and therefore increased risk for DoD. Outsourcing and complex domestic and foreign corporate mergers and acquisitions have made it even more difficult for DoD to be assured that its prime contractors' second-, third-, and fourth-tier subcontractors understand its security requirements and are prepared to support them in a national emergency.

Defense Industrial Base Challenges

Over the past 20 years, DoD's dependency on the private sector has greatly increased. Outsourcing has caused the department to rely increasingly on contractors to perform many of the tasks that were once under the exclusive purview and control of the military. Even the utilities that service many of the nation's important military installations are being privatized. Because of market competition and attrition, DoD now relies more and more on a single or very limited number of private-sector suppliers to fulfill some of its most essential needs. DoD, unlike other federal government agencies, requires strict adherence to military product specification and unique requirements for services. Select private-industry vendors may be the only

suppliers in the world capable of satisfying these unique requirements. Many of these sources have single manufacturing and distribution points that warrant additional security review and assessment.

A related problem involves the current process through which DoD contracts with the private sector to provide critical services and supplies. Most often the procurement process is based on cost and efficiency. Such an approach may not always take into account the vendor's critical infrastructure protection practices (e.g., workforce hiring, supplier base) and its ability to supply products and services and provide surge response during an emergency or exigent circumstances.

Finally, there are also growing concerns within the private sector regarding the potential for additional costs and risks resulting from federal mandates that require private industry to implement enhanced infrastructure protection measures.

Defense Industrial Base Initiatives

The infrastructures of the private defense industry and DoD are already integrated on many levels. DoD, in concert with DHS, will continue working with the private sector to identify critical installations and infrastructures, and, subsequently, to delineate specific protection requirements. Furthermore, DoD and DHS will collaborate with key defense industrial base

organizations to integrate and build upon their individual existing protection plans.

Additional defense industrial base protection initiatives include efforts to:

Build critical infrastructure protection requirements into contract processes and procedures

DoD will collaborate with the defense industry to review contract processes and procedures to determine how to include provisions that address critical infrastructure protection needs. Contracts will specifically address national emergency situation requirements, such as contractor response times, supply and labor availability, and direct logistic support. When appropriate, contracts will also include language regarding program manager accountability for the protection of supporting infrastructures. Sensitive contractual documents will receive greater scrutiny and revision prior to public posting. Additionally, DoD will give specific scrutiny to its potential dependency on foreign commercial operators and suppliers.

Incorporate security concerns into production and distribution processes and procedures

DoD and industry will explore ways to eliminate key production and distribution bottlenecks.

Develop an effective means of sharing security-related information between defense organizations and private-sector service providers

DoD will work with DHS and the intelligence and law enforcement communities to establish the necessary policies and mechanisms to facilitate a productive exchange of security-related information with the defense industry.

TELECOMMUNICATIONS

The composition of the telecommunications sector evolves continuously due to technology advances, business and competitive pressures, and changes in the regulatory environment. Despite its dynamic nature, the sector has consistently provided robust and reliable communications and processes to meet the needs of businesses and governments. In the new threat environment, the sector faces significant challenges to protect its vast and dispersed critical assets, both cyber and physical. Because the government and critical-infrastructure industries rely heavily on the public telecommunications infrastructure for vital communications services, the sector's protection initiatives are particularly important.

The telecommunications sector provides voice and data service to public and private users through a complex and diverse public-network infrastructure encompassing the Public Switched Telecommunications Network (PSTN), the Internet, and private enterprise networks. The PSTN provides switched circuits for telephone, data, and leased point-to-point services. It consists of physical facilities, including over 20,000 switches, access tandems, and other equipment. These components are connected by nearly two billion miles of fiber and copper cable. The physical PSTN remains the backbone of the infrastructure, with cellular, microwave, and satellite technologies providing extended gateways to the wireline network for mobile users. Supporting the underlying PSTN are Operations, Administration, Maintenance, and Provisioning systems, which provide the vital management and administrative functions, such as billing, accounting, configuration, and security management.

Advances in data network technology and the increasing demand for data services have spawned the rapid proliferation of the Internet infrastructure. The Internet consists of a global network of packet-switched networks that use a common suite of protocols. Internet Service Providers (ISPs) provide end-users with access to the Internet. Larger ISPs use Network Operation Centers (NOCs) to manage their high capacity networks, linking them through Internet peering points or network access points. Smaller ISPs usually lease their long-haul transmission capacity from the larger ISPs and provide regional and local Internet access to end-users via the PSTN. Internet access providers interconnect with the PSTN through points of presence, typically a switch or a router, located at carrier central offices. International PSTN and Internet traffic travels via underwater cables that reach the United States at various cable landing points.

In addition to the PSTN and the Internet, enterprise networks are an important component of the telecommunications infrastructure. Enterprise networks are dedicated networks supporting the voice and data needs and operations of large enterprises. These networks comprise a combination of leased lines or services from the PSTN or Internet providers.

The Telecommunications Act of 1996 opened local PSTN service to competition. It required incumbent carriers to allow their competitors to have open access to their networks. As a result, carriers began to concentrate their assets in collocation facilities and other buildings known as telecom hotels, collocation sites, or peering points instead of laying down new cable. ISPs also gravitated to these facilities to reduce the costs of exchanging traffic with other ISPs. Open competition, therefore, has caused the operation of the PSTN and the Internet (including switching, transport, signaling, routing, control, security, and management) to become increasingly interconnected, software driven, and remotely managed, while the industry's physical assets are increasingly concentrated in shared facilities.

The telecommunications infrastructure is undergoing a significant transformation that involves the convergence of traditional circuit-switched networks with broadband packet-based IP networks, including the Internet. Eventually, the packet networks will subsume the circuit-switched networks, leading to the establishment of a public, broadband, diverse, and scaleable packet-based network known as the Next Generation Network (NGN). Additionally, the evolution of the telecommunications infrastructure has included steady growth in mobile wireless services and applications. Wireless telecommunications providers transmit messages using an infrastructure of base stations and radio-cell towers located throughout the wireless provider's service area. Wireless services consist of digital mobile phones and emerging data services, including Internet communications, wireless local-area networks, and advanced telephony services.

Convergence, the growth of the NGN, and emergence of new wireless capabilities continue to introduce new physical components to the telecommunications infrastructure. Government and industry consistently work together to develop strategies to ensure that the evolving infrastructure remains reliable, robust, and secure. Public-private partnerships and organizations currently addressing telecommunications security include the President's National Security Telecommunications Advisory Committee and Critical Infrastructure Protection Board (PCIPB), the Government Network Security Information Exchanges, the Telecommunications ISAC, and the Network Reliability and Interoperability Council of the FCC. Recommendations by these bodies and collaboration among industry and government will shape the security and reliability of the evolving infrastructure.

Telecommunications Sector Challenges

Every day the sector must contend with traditional natural and human-based threats to its physical infrastructure, such as weather events, unintentional cable cuts, and the insider threat (e.g., physical and cyber sabotage). The September 11 attacks revealed the threat terrorism poses to the telecommunications sector's physical infrastructure. While it was not a direct target of the attacks, the telecommunications sector suffered significant collateral damage. In the future, certain concentrations of key sector assets themselves could become attractive direct targets for terrorists, particularly with the increased use of collocation facilities. The telecommunications infrastructure withstood the September 11 attacks in overall terms and demonstrated remarkable resiliency because damage to telecommunications assets at the attack sites was offset by diverse, redundant, and multifaceted communications capabilities.

Priorities for telecommunications carriers are service reliability, cost balancing, security, and effective risk management postures. The government places high priority on the consistent application of security across the infrastructure. Although private- and public-sector

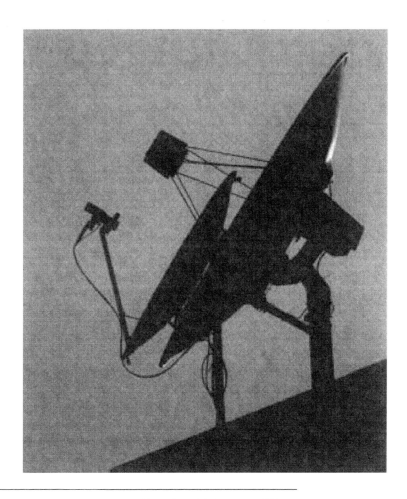

stakeholders share similar objectives, they have different perspectives on what constitutes acceptable risk and how to achieve security and reliability. Therefore, an agreement on a sustainable security threshold and corresponding security requirements remains elusive.

Because of growing interdependencies among the various critical infrastructures, a direct or indirect attack on any of them could result in cascading effects across the others. Such interdependencies increase the need to identify critical assets and secure them against both physical and cyber threats. Critical infrastructures rely upon a secure and robust telecommunications infrastructure. Redundancy within the infrastructure is critical to ensure that single points of failure in one infrastructure will not adversely impact others. It is vital that government and industry work together to characterize the state of diversity in the telecommunications architecture. They must also collaborate to understand the topography of the physical components of the architecture to establish a foundation for defining a strategy to ensure physical and logical diversity.

Despite significant challenges, the telecommunications marketplace remains competitive, and customer demand for services is steady, if not increasing. An economic upturn within the industry could rapidly accelerate service demands. The interplay of market forces and FCC oversight will ensure the continuance of service delivery to sustain critical telecommunications functions. Nevertheless, recent economic distress has forced companies to spend their existing resources on basic network operations rather than re-capitalizing, securing, and enhancing the infrastructure, which could amplify the financial impact of necessary infrastructure protection investments.

Telecommunications Sector Initiatives

Given the reality of the physical and cyber threats to the telecommunications sector, government and industry must continue to work together to understand vulnerabilities, develop countermeasures, establish policies and procedures, and raise awareness necessary to mitigate risks. The telecommunications sector has a long, successful history of collaboration with government to address concerns over the reliability and security of the telecommunications infrastructure.

The sector has recently undertaken a variety of new initiatives to further ensure both reliability and quick recovery and reconstitution. Within this environment of increasing emphasis on protection issues, public-private partnership can be further leveraged to address a number of key telecommunications initiatives, including efforts to:

Define an appropriate threshold for security

DHS will work with industry to define an appropriate security threshold for the sector and develop a set of requirements derived from that definition. DHS will work with industry to close the gap between respective security expectations and requirements. Reaching agreement on a methodology for ensuring physical diversity is a key element of this effort.

Expand infrastructure diverse routing capability

DHS will leverage and enhance the government's capabilities to define and map the overall telecommunications architecture. This effort will identify critical intersections among the various infrastructures and lead to strategies that better address security and reliability.

Understand the risks associated with vulnerabilities of the telecommunications infrastructure

The telecommunications infrastructure, including the PSTN, the Internet, and enterprise networks, provides essential communications for governments at all levels and other critical infrastructures. DHS will work with the private sector to conduct studies to understand physical vulnerabilities within the telecommunications infrastructure and their associated risks. Studies will focus on facilities where many different types of equipment and multiple carriers are concentrated.

Coordinate with key allies and trading partners

More than ever our Nation has a common reliance on vital communications circuits and processes with our key allies and trading partners. DHS will work with other nations to consider innovative communications paths that provide priority communications processes to link our governments, global industries, and networks in such a manner that vital communications are assured.

ENERGY

Energy drives the foundation of many of the sophisticated processes at work in American society today. It is essential to our economy, national defense, and quality of life.

The energy sector is commonly divided into two segments in the context of critical infrastructure protection: electricity and oil and natural gas. The electric industry services almost 130 million households and institutions. The United States consumed nearly 3.6 trillion kilowatt hours in 2001. Oil and natural gas facilities and assets[1] are widely distributed, consisting of more than 300.000 producing sites, 4,000 off-shore platforms, more than 600 natural gas processing plants, 153 refineries, and more than 1.400 product terminals, and 7,500 bulk stations.

ELECTRICITY

Almost every form of productive activity—whether in businesses, manufacturing plants, schools, hospitals, or homes—requires electricity. Electricity is also necessary to produce other forms of energy, such as refined oil. Were a widespread or long-term disruption of the power grid to occur, many of the activities critical to our economy and national defense—including those associated with response and recovery—would be impossible.

The North American electric system is an interconnected, multi-nodal distribution system that accounts for virtually all the electricity supplied to the United States, Canada, and a portion of Baja California Norte, Mexico. The physical system consists of three major parts: generation, transmission and distribution, and control and communications.

Generation assets include fossil fuel plants, hydroelectric dams, and nuclear power plants. Transmission and distribution systems link areas of the national grid. Distribution systems manage and control the distribution of electricity into homes and businesses. Control and communications systems operate and monitor critical infrastructure components.

In addition to these components, the electric infrastructure also comprises ancillary facilities and systems that guarantee fuel supplies necessary to support electricity generation, some of which involve the handling of hazardous materials. The electricity sector also depends heavily on other critical infrastructures for power generation, such as telecommunications and transportation.

The North American electric system is the world's most reliable, a fact that can be attributed to industry-led efforts to identify single points of failure and system interdependencies, and institute appropriate back-up processes, systems, and facilities.

After New York's power blackout in 1965, the industry established the North American Electric Reliability Council (NERC) to develop guidelines and procedures for preventing similar incidents. NERC is a nonprofit corporation made up of 10 regional reliability councils, whose voluntary membership represents all segments of the electricity industry, including public and private utilities from the U.S. and Canada. Through NERC, the electricity sector coordinates programs to enhance security for the electricity industry.

The electricity sector is highly regulated even as the industry is being restructured to increase competition. The Federal Energy Regulatory Commission (FERC) and state utility regulatory commissions regulate some of the activities and operations of certain electricity industry participants. The Nuclear Regulatory Commission (NRC) regulates nuclear power reactors and other civilian nuclear facilities, materials, and activities.[2]

Electricity Sector Challenges

The electricity sector is highly complex, and its numerous component assets and systems span the North American continent. Many of the sector's key assets, such as generation facilities, key substations, and switchyards, present unique protection challenges.

Increased competition and structural changes currently taking place within the sector may alter security incentives and responsibilities of electricity market participants. These stakeholders are diverse in size, capabilities, and focus. Currently, individual companies pay for levels of protection that are consistent with their resources and customer expectations. Typically, these companies seek to recover the costs of new security investments through proposed rate or price increases. Under current federal law, however, there is no assurance that electricity industry participants would be allowed to recover the costs of federally mandated security measures through such rate or price increases.

Another challenge for the electricity industry is effective, sector-wide communications. The owners and operators of the electric system are a large and heterogeneous group. Industry associations serve as clearing houses for industry-related information, but not all industry owners and operators belong to such organizations. Data needed to perform thorough analyses on the infrastructure's interdependencies is not readily available. A focused analysis of time-phased effects of one infrastructure on another, including loss of operations metrics, would help identify dependencies and establish protection priorities and strategies.

For certain transmission and distribution facilities, providing redundancy and increasing generating capacity provide greater reliability of electricity service. However, this approach faces several challenges. Long lead times, possible denials of rights-of-way, state and local siting requirements, "not-in-my-backyard" community perspectives, and uncertain rates of return when compared to competing investment needs are hurdles that may prevent owners and operators of electricity facilities from investing sufficiently in security and service assurance measures.

Building a less vulnerable grid represents another option for protecting the national electricity infrastructure. Work is ongoing to develop a national R&D strategy for the electricity sector. Additionally, FERC has developed R&D guidelines, and the Department of Energy's (DoE's) National Grid Study contains recommendations focused on enhancing physical and cyber security for the transmission system.

Electricity Sector Initiatives

The electricity industry has a history of taking proactive measures to assure the reliability and availability of the electricity system. Individual enterprises also work actively in their communities to address public safety issues related to their systems and facilities. Since September 11, 2001, the sector has reviewed its security guidelines and initiated a series of intra-industry working groups to address specific aspects of security. It has created a utility-sector security committee at the chief executive officer level to enhance planning, awareness, and resource allocation within the industry.

The sector as a whole, with NERC as the sector coordinator, has been working in collaboration with DOE since 1998 to assess its risk posture in light of the new threat environment, particularly with respect to the electric system's dependence on information technology and networks. In the process, the sector has created an awareness program that includes a *"Business Case for Action"* for industry senior executives, a strategic reference document, *"An Approach to Action for the Electric Power Sector,"* and security guidelines related to physical and cyber security.

With respect to managing security information, the sector has established an indications, analysis, and warning program that trains utilities on incident reporting and alert notification procedures. The sector has also developed threat alert levels for both physical and cyber events, which include action-response guidelines for each alert level. The industry has also established an ISAC to gather incident information, relay alert notices, and coordinate daily briefs between the federal government and electric grid operators around the country.

Power management control rooms are probably the most protected aspect of the electrical network. NERC's guidelines require a backup system and/or manual work-arounds to bypass damaged systems. FERC is also working with the sector to develop a common set of security requirements for all enterprises in the competitive electric supply market.

Additional electricity sector protection initiatives include efforts to:

Identify equipment stock pile requirements
DHS and DoE will work with the electricity sector to inventory components and equipment critical to electric-system operations and to identify and assess other approaches to enhance restoration and recovery to include standardizing equipment and increasing component interchangeability.

Re-evaluate and adjust nationwide protection planning, system restoration, and recovery in response to attacks

The electric power industry has an excellent process and record of reconstitution and recovery from disruptive events. Jointly, industry and government need to evaluate this system and its processes to support the evolution from a local and regional system to an integrated national response system. DHS and DoE will work with the electricity sector to ensure that existing coordination and mutual aid processes can effectively and efficiently support protection, response, and recovery activities as the structure of the electricity sector continues to evolve.

Develop strategies to reduce vulnerabilities

DHS and DoE will work with state and local governments and the electric power industry to identify the appropriate levels of redundancy of critical parts of the electric system, as well as requirements for designing and implementing redundancy in view of the industry's realignment and restructuring activities.

Develop standardized guidelines for physical security programs

DHS and DOE will work with the sector to define consistent criteria for criticality, standard approaches for vulnerability and risk assessments for critical facilities, and physical security training for electricity sector personnel.

OIL & NATURAL GAS

The oil and natural gas industries are closely integrated. The oil infrastructure consists of five general components: oil production, crude oil transport, refining, product transport and distribution, and control and other external support systems. Oil and natural gas production include: exploration, field development, on- and offshore production, field collection systems, and their supporting infrastructures. Crude oil transport includes pipelines (160,000 miles), storage terminals, ports, and ships. The refinement infrastructure consists of about 150 refineries that range in size and production capabilities from 5,000 to over 500,000 barrels per day. Transport and distribution of oil includes pipelines, trains, ships, ports, terminals and storage, trucks, and retail stations.

The natural gas industry consists of three major components: exploration and production, transmission, and local distribution. The U.S. produces roughly 20 percent of the world's natural gas supply. There are 278,000 miles of natural gas pipelines and 1,119,000 miles of natural gas distribution lines in the U.S.

Distribution includes storage facilities, gas processing, liquid natural gas facilities, pipelines, citygates, and liquefied petroleum gas storage facilities. Citygates are distribution pipeline nodes through which gas passes from interstate pipelines to a local distribution system. Natural gas storage refers to underground aquifers, depleted oil and gas fields, and salt caverns.

The pipeline and distribution segments of the oil and natural gas industries are highly regulated. Oversight includes financial, safety, and siting regulations. The exploration and production side of the industry is less regulated, but is affected by safety regulations and restrictions concerning property access.

Oil and Natural Gas Sector Challenges

Protection of critical assets requires both heightened security awareness and investment in protective equipment and systems. One serious issue is the lack of metrics to determine and justify corporate security expenditures. In the case of natural disasters or accidents, there are well-established methods for determining risks and cost-effective levels of investments in protective equipment, systems, and methods for managing risk (e.g., insurance). It is not clear what levels of security and protection are appropriate and cost effective to meet the risks of terrorist attack.

The first government responders to a terrorist attack on most oil and natural gas sector facilities will be local police and fire departments. In general, these responders need to improve their capabilities and preparedness to confront well-planned, sophisticated attacks, particularly those involving CBR weapons. Fortunately, because of public-safety requirements related to their operations and facilities, the oil and natural gas industries have substantial protection programs already in place.

Quick action to repair damaged infrastructure in an emergency can be impeded by a number of hurdles, including the long lead time needed to obtain local, state, and federal construction permits or waivers; requirements for environmental reviews and impact statements; and lengthy processes for obtaining construction rights-of-way for the placement of pipelines on adjoining properties if a new path becomes necessary. The availability of necessary materials and equipment, and the uniqueness of such equipment are also impediments to rapid reconstitution of damaged infrastructure.

The current system for locating and distributing replacement parts needs to be enhanced significantly. The components themselves range from state-of-the-art systems to mechanisms that are decades old. While

newer systems are standardized, many of the older components are unique and must be custom-manufactured. Moreover, there is extensive variation in size, ownership, and security across natural gas facilities. There are also a large number of natural gas facilities scattered over broad geographical areas—a fact that complicates protection.

Oil and Natural Gas Sector Initiatives

Oil and natural gas sector protection initiatives include efforts to:

Plan and invest in research and development for the oil and gas industry to enhance robustness and reliability

Utilizing the federal government's national scientific and research capabilities, DHS and DoE will work with oil and natural gas sector stakeholders to develop an appropriate strategy for research and development to support protection, response, and recovery requirements.

Develop strategies to reduce vulnerabilities

DHS and DoE will work with state and local governments and industry to identify the appropriate levels of redundancy of critical components and systems, as well as requirements for designing and enhancing reliability.

Develop standardized guidelines for physical security programs

DHS and DoE will work with the oil and natural gas industry representatives to define consistent criteria for criticality, standard approaches for

vulnerability and risk assessments for various facilities, and physical security training for industry personnel.

Develop guidelines for measures to reconstitute capabilities of individual facilities and systems

DHS and DoE will convene an advisory task force of industry representatives from the sector, construction firms, equipment suppliers, oil-engineering firms, state and local governments, and federal agencies to identify appropriate planning requirements and approaches.

Develop a national system for locating and distributing critical components in support of response and recovery activities

DHS and DoE will work with industry to develop regional and national programs for identifying spare parts, requirements, notifying parties of their availability, and distributing them in an emergency.

---

1   Pipelines that transport oil and gas supplies are components of the transportation sector's critical infrastructure and are regulated by the Department of Transportation (DoT) for safety purposes. Their protection is discussed in further detail on pages 58-59 of the *Transportation Sector Section* of this document.

2   Nuclear power plants are an important component of the energy sector's critical infrastructure. Because of the potential public health and safety consequences an attack on a nuclear facility could cause, specific issues related to their protection are included on page 74 of the *Protecting Key Assets* chapter of this document.

TRANSPORTATION

The transportation sector consists of several key modes: aviation, maritime traffic, rail, pipelines, highways, trucking and busing, and public mass transit. The diversity and size of the transportation sector makes it vital to our economy and national security, including military mobilization and deployment. As a whole, its infrastructure is robust, having been developed over decades of both private and public investment. Together the various transportation modes provide mobility of our population and contribute to our much-cherished individual freedom. The transportation infrastructure is also convenient. Americans rely on its easy access and reliability in their daily lives.

Interdependencies exist between transportation and nearly every other sector of the economy. Consequently, a threat to the transportation sector may impact other industries that rely on it. Threat information affecting transportation modes must be adequately addressed through communication and coordination among multiple parties who use or rely on these systems.

AVIATION

The aviation mode is vast, consisting of thousands of entry points. It also has symbolic value, representing the freedom of movement that Americans value so highly as well as the technological and industrial

prowess that have made the United States a world power. The Nation's aviation system consists of two main parts:

- Airports and the associated assets needed to support their operations, including the aircraft that they serve; and

- Aviation command, control, communications, and information systems needed to support and maintain safe use of our national airspace.

Before September 11, the security of airports and their associated assets was the responsibility of private carriers and state and local airport owners and operators. In the months following the September 11 attacks, Congress passed legislation establishing the Transportation Security Administration as the responsible authority for assuring aviation security.

Aviation Mode Challenges

As the events of September 11 illustrated, aviation's vital importance to the U.S. economy and the freedom it provides our citizens make its protection an important national priority. Aviation faces several unique protection challenges. Its distribution and open access through thousands of entry points at home and abroad make it difficult to secure. Furthermore, components of the aviation infrastructure are not only attractive

terrorist targets, but also serve as potential weapons to be exploited. Together, these factors make the U.S. aviation infrastructure a potential target for future terrorist strikes.

Additional unique protection challenges for aviation include:

- *Volume:* U.S. air carriers transport millions of passengers every day and at least twice as many bags and other cargo.

- *Limited capabilities and available space:* Current detection equipment and methods are limited in number, capability, and ease of use.

- *Time-sensitive cargo:* "Just-in-time" delivery of valuable cargo is essential for many businesses—any significant time delay in processing and transporting such cargo would negatively affect the U.S. economy.

- *Security versus convenience:* Maintaining security while limiting congestion and delays complicates the task of security and has important financial implications.

- *Accessibility:* Most airports are open to the public; their facilities are close to public roadways for convenience and to streamline access for vehicles delivering passengers to terminals.

Another concern for the aviation industry is the additional cost of increased security during sustained periods of heightened alert. Since September 11, 2001, airports across the country have-in effect-been working at surge capacity to meet the security requirements of the current threat environment. Some cash-strapped operators must now balance providing higher levels of security with staying in business.

Aviation Mode Initiatives

Airport security failures on September 11 have placed the aviation industry under intense public scrutiny. To regain the public's confidence in air travel, public and private organizations have made substantial investments to increase airport security. Much work remains. DHS, as the federal lead department for the transportation sector, will work with DoT, industry, and state and local governments to organize, plan, and implement needed protection activities.

Aviation mode protection initiatives include efforts to:

Identify vulnerabilities, interdependencies, and remediation requirements

DHS and DoT will work with representatives from state and local governments and industry to implement or facilitate risk assessments to identify

vulnerabilities, interdependencies, and remediation requirements for operations and coordination-center facilities and systems, such as the need for redundant telecommunications for air traffic command and control centers.

Identify potential threats to passengers

DHS and DoT will work with airline and airport security executives to develop or facilitate new methods for identifying likely human threats while respecting constitutional freedoms and privacy.

Improve security at key points of access

DHS and DoT will work with airline and airport security executives to tighten security or facilitate increased security at restricted access points within airport terminal areas, as well as the perimeter of airports and associated facilities, including operations and coordination centers.

Increase cargo screening capabilities

DHS and DoT will work with airline and airport security officials to identify and implement or facilitate technologies and processes to enhance airport baggage-screening capacities.

Identify and improve detection technologies

DHS and DoT will work with airline and airport security executives to implement or facilitate enhanced technologies for detecting explosives. Such devices will mitigate the impact of increased security on passenger check-in efficiency and convenience, and also provide a more effective and efficient means of assuring vital aviation security.

PASSENGER RAIL AND RAILROADS

During every hour of every day, trains traverse the United States, linking producers of raw materials to manufacturers and retailers. They carry mining, manufacturing, and agriculture products; liquid chemicals and fuels; and consumer goods. Trains carry 40 percent of intercity freight—a much larger portion than is moved by any other single mode of transportation. About 20 percent of that freight is coal, a critical resource for the generation of electricity. More than 20 million intercity travelers use the rail system annually, and 45 million passengers ride trains and subways operated by local transit authorities. Securing rail-sector assets is critical to protecting U.S. commerce and the safety of travelers.

Rail Mode Challenges

Our Nation's railway system is vast and complex, with multiple points of entry. Differences in design, structure, and purpose of railway stations complicate the sector's overall protection framework. The size and breadth of the sector make it difficult to react to threats effectively or efficiently in all scenarios. This fact complicates protection efforts, but it also offers certain mitigating potential in the event of a terrorist attack. For example, trains are confined to specific routes and are highly controllable. If hijacked, a train can be shunted off the mainline and rendered less of a threat. Similarly, the loss of a bridge or tunnel can

impact traffic along major corridors; however, the potential for national-level disruptions is limited.

The greater risk is associated with rail transport of hazardous materials. Freight railways often carry hazardous materials that are essential to other sectors and public services. The decision-making process regarding their transport is complex and requires close coordination between industry and government. A sector-wide information sharing process could help prevent over-reactive security measures, such as restricting the shipment of critical hazardous materials nationwide as a blanket safety measure in response to a localized incident.

Security solutions to the container shipping challenge should recognize that, in many cases, commerce, including essential national security materials, must continue to flow. Stifling commerce to meet security needs simply swaps one consequence of a security threat for another. In the event that a credible threat were to necessitate a shutdown, well-developed continuity of operations procedures can mitigate further unintentional negative consequences. For example, contingency planning can help determine how quickly commerce can be resumed; whether rerouting provides a measure of protection; or what specific shipments should be exempt from a shutdown, such as national defense critical materials.

An additional area of concern is the marking of container cars to indicate the specific type of hazardous materials being transported. During an emergency response, placards on rail cars help to alert first responders to hazardous materials they may encounter. Planners must take care, however, to devise a system of markings that terrorists cannot easily decipher.

Like the aviation sector, the rail industry also faces the additional costs of sustaining increased security during periods of heightened alert. Since the events of September 11, the railroads across the country have—in effect—been working at surge capacity to meet the security requirements of the increased threat environment, which entails assigning overtime and hiring temporary security personnel. Such reservoirs of capacity are costly to maintain. Nevertheless, the rail sector has had to adopt these heightened security levels as the new "normal" state. Some cash-strapped operators now face trade-offs between providing increased levels of security and going out of business.

Railroads have well-developed contingency plans and backups for dispatch, control, and communications equipment that are sufficient for localized or minor disruptions. Developing this type of backup to enable

continuation of operations after a cataclysmic event is problematic given the costs associated with extensive structural enhancements.

Rail Mode Initiatives

The rail mode has been working actively with DoT to assess the risk environment. As a result, it has developed a comprehensive modal risk assessment and established a surface transportation ISAC to facilitate the exchange of information related to both cyber and physical threats specific to the railroads.

Since September 11, many rail operators have added investments to their security programs. Additional rail mode protection initiatives include efforts to:

Develop improved decision-making criteria regarding the shipment of hazardous materials

DHS and DoT, coordinating with other federal agencies, state and local governments, and industry will facilitate the development of an improved process to assure informed decision-making with respect to hazardous materials shipment.

Develop technologies and procedures to screen intermodal containers and passenger baggage

DHS and DoT will work with sector counterparts to identify and explore technologies and processes to enable efficient and expeditious screening of rail passengers and baggage, especially at intermodal stations.

Improve security of intermodal transportation

DHS and DoT will work with sector counterparts to identify and facilitate the development of technologies and procedures to secure inter-modal containers and detect threatening content.

DHS and DoT will also work with the rail industry to devise or enable a hazardous materials identification system that supports the needs of first responders, yet avoids providing terrorists with easy identification of a potential weapon.

Clearly delineate roles and responsibilities regarding surge requirements

DHS and DoT will work with industry to delineate infrastructure protection roles and responsibilities to enable the rail industry to address surge requirements for resources in the case of catastrophic events.

Costs and resource allocation remains a contentious issue for the rail sector. DHS and DoT will also convene a working group consisting of government and industry representatives to identify options for the implementation of surge capabilities, including access to federal facilities and capabilities in extreme emergencies.

HIGHWAYS, TRUCKING, AND BUSING

The trucking and busing industry is a fundamental component of our national transportation infrastructure. Without the sector's resources, the movement of people, goods, and services around the country would be greatly impeded. Components of this infrastructure include highways, roads, inter-modal terminals, bridges, tunnels, trucks, buses, maintenance facilities, and roadway border crossings.

Highways, Trucking, and Busing Mode Challenges

Because of its heterogeneity in size and operations and the multitude of owners and operators nationwide, the trucking and busing infrastructure is highly resilient, flexible, and responsive to market demand. For the same reason, the sector is fractionated and regulated by multiple jurisdictions at state, federal, and—sometimes—local levels. The size and pervasive nature of the trucking and busing infrastructure pose significant protection challenges.

Transportation choke points (e.g., bridges and tunnels, inter-modal terminals, border crossings, and highway interchanges) present unique protection challenges. Overall understanding of infrastructure choke points is limited. Common criteria for identifying critical choke points are therefore difficult to establish. We must undertake a comprehensive, systematic effort to identify key assets, particularly those whose destruction or

disruption would entail significant public health and safety consequences or significant economic impact.

Although many states have conducted risk assessments of their respective highway infrastructures, no true basis for comparison among them exists to determine relative criticality. Likewise, there is no coordinated mechanism for assessing choke-point vulnerabilities or conducting and evaluating risk mitigation planning. A major reason for this lack of synchronization within the sector is a paucity of funds to promote communication among industry members and facilitate cooperation for joint protection planning efforts. As a result, the sector as a whole has neither a coherent picture of industry-wide risks, nor a set of appropriate security criteria on which to baseline its protection planning efforts, such as what conditions constitute threats for the sector, or standards for infrastructure protection or threat reduction. The sector's diverse and widely distributed constituency complicates this situation.

Given the number of public and private small-business owners and operators in this sector, the cost of infrastructure protection is also a major challenge. Like the rail mode, in addition to the financial concerns associated with new security investments, highway, trucking, and busing organizations also regard the possibility of security-related delays at border crossings as a potential problem of major financial significance.

Another challenge is the way in which sector security incidents are handled across multiple jurisdictions. Because different law enforcement agencies differ in their approaches to crimes like truck theft, law enforcement responses to security incidents in this sector are inconsistent across jurisdictional lines.

Highways, Trucking, and Busing Mode Initiatives

Like the other major transportation modes, the highways, trucking, and busing mode has assessed its own security programs in light of the September 11 attacks. However, the sector's vast, heterogeneous nature requires further expanded coordination among stakeholder organizations to assure a more consistent, integrated national approach. Additionally, a better understanding of the overall system would lead to more adaptable, less intrusive, and more cost-effective security processes. Highways, trucking, and busing protection initiatives include efforts to:

Facilitate comprehensive risk, threat, and vulnerability assessments

DHS, working closely with DoT and other key sector stakeholders, will facilitate comprehensive risk, threat, and vulnerability assessments for this mode.

Develop guidelines and standard criteria for identifying and mitigating chokepoints

DHS, working with DoT and other sector key stakeholders, will develop guidelines and standard criteria for identifying and mitigating choke points, both nationally and regionally.

Harden industry infrastructure against terrorism through technology

DHS will work jointly with industry and state and local governments to explore and identify potential technology solutions and standards that will support analysis and afford better and more cost effective protection against terrorism.

Create national transportation operator security education and awareness programs

DHS and DoT will work with industry to create national operator security education and awareness programs to provide the foundation for greater cooperation and coordination within this highly diverse mode.

PIPELINES

The United States has a vast pipeline industry, consisting of many hundreds of thousands of miles of pipelines, many of which are buried underground. These lines move a variety of substances such as crude oil, refined petroleum products, and natural gas.

Pipeline facilities already incorporate a variety of stringent safety precautions that account for the potential effects a disaster could have on surrounding areas. Moreover, most elements of pipeline infrastructures can be quickly repaired or bypassed to mitigate localized disruptions. Destruction of one or even several of its key components would not disrupt the entire system. As a whole, the response and recovery capabilities of the pipeline industry are well proven, and most large control-center operators have established extensive contingency plans and backup protocols.

Pipeline Mode Challenges

Pipelines are not independent entities, but rather integral parts of industrial and public service networks. Loss of a pipeline could impact a wide array of facilities and industrial factories that depend on reliable fuel delivery to operate.

Several hundred thousand miles of pipeline span the country, and it is not realistic to expect total security for all facilities. As such, protection efforts focus on infrastructure components whose impairment would have significant effects on the energy markets and the economy as a whole. For the pipeline industry,

determining *what* to protect and *when* to protect it is a factor in cost-effective infrastructure protection. During periods of high demand—such as the winter months—pipeline systems typically operate at peak capacity and are more important to the facilities and functions they serve.

The pipeline industry as a whole has an excellent safety record, as well as in-place crisis management protocols to manage disruptions as they occur. Nevertheless, many of the products that pipelines deliver are inherently volatile. Hence, their protection is a significant issue.

Pipelines cross numerous state and local, as well as international jurisdictions. The number and variety of stakeholders create a confusing, and sometimes conflicting, array of regulations and security programs for the industry to manage, especially with respect to the ability of pipeline facilities to recover, reconstitute, and re-establish service quickly after a disruption.

The pipeline industry's increasing interdependencies with the energy and telecommunications sectors necessitate cooperation with other critical infrastructures during protection and response planning. Individually, companies have difficulty assessing the broader implications of an attack on their critical facilities. These interdependencies call for cross-sector coordination for to be truly responsive to national concerns. Additionally, some issues concerning recovery or reconstitution will require at least regional planning within the industry, as well as the sharing of sensitive business information that may run into proprietary concerns.

Pipeline Mode Initiatives

Historically, individual enterprises within this sector have invested in the security of their facilities to protect their ability to deliver oil and gas products. Representatives from major entities within this sector have examined the new terrorist risk environment. As a result, they have developed a plan for action, including industry-wide information sharing. In addition to industry efforts, DoT has developed a methodology for determining pipeline facility criticality and a system of recommended protective measures that are synchronized with the threat levels of the Homeland Security Advisory System. Additional pipeline mode protection initiatives include efforts to:

Develop standard reconstitution protocols
> DHS, in collaboration with DoE, DoT, and industry, will initiate a study to identify, clarify, and establish authorities and procedures as needed to reconstitute facilities as quickly as possible after a disruption.

Develop standard security assessment and threat deterrent guidelines
> DHS, in collaboration with DoE and DoT, will work with state and local governments and the pipeline industry to develop consensus security guidance on assessing vulnerabilities, improving security plans, implementing specific deterrent and protective actions, and upgrading response and recovery plans for pipelines.

Work with other sectors to manage risks resulting from interdependencies
> DHS, in collaboration with DoE and DoT, will convene cross-sector working groups to develop models for integrating protection priorities and emergency response plans.

MARITIME

The maritime shipping infrastructure includes ports and their associated assets, ships and passenger transportation systems, costal and inland waterways, locks, dams and canals, and the network of railroads and pipelines that connect these waterborne systems to other transportation networks. There are 361 seaports in the United States, and their operations range widely in size and characteristics.

Most ports have diverse waterside facilities that are owned, operated, and accessed by diverse entities. State and local governments control some port authority facilities, while others are owned and operated by private corporations. Most ships are privately owned and operated. Cargo is stored in terminals at ports and loaded onto ships or other vehicles that pass through on their way to domestic and international destinations. DoD has also designated certain commercial seaports as strategic seaports, which provide facilities and services needed for military deployment.

Maritime Mode Challenges

The size, diversity, and complexity of this infrastructure make the inspection of all vessels and cargo that passes through our ports an extremely difficult undertaking. Current inspection methods—both physical and technological—are limited and costly. As with other modes

of transportation that cross international borders, we must manage the tension between efficient processing of cargo and passengers and adequate security.

Major portions of the maritime industry's operations are international in nature and are governed by international agreements and multinational authorities, such as the International Maritime Organization. Negotiation of maritime rules and practices with foreign governments lies within the purview of DoS. Often these international efforts involve extended negotiation timelines.

DoT currently recommends guidelines for passenger vessel and terminal security, including passenger and baggage screening and training of crews. The industry requires R&D for cost-effective technologies for the rapid detection of explosives and other hazardous substances, as well as for new vessel designs to minimize the likelihood of a ship sinking if it were attacked.

Much of the port system represents a significant protection challenge, particularly in the case of high consequence cargo. Physical and operational security guidelines have undergone a comprehensive review, from which DoT and DHS will issue guidance and recommendations for appropriate protective actions. Efforts to increase the security of the maritime industry must also consider infrastructures subject to

multi-agency jurisdictions and the international framework in which the industry operates.

Maritime Mode Initiatives

Following the September 11 attacks, initial risk assessments were conducted for all ports. These assessments have helped refine critical infrastructure and key asset designations, assess vulnerabilities, guide the development of mitigation strategies, and illuminate best practices. Most port authorities and private facility owners have also reexamined their security practices. Based on these preliminary risk assessments, DoT increased vessel notification requirements to shift limited resources to maintain positive control of movement of high-risk vessels carrying high-consequence cargoes and large numbers of passengers. DoT and the U.S. Coast Guard have also established a Sea Marshal program and deployable Maritime Safety and Security Teams to implement these activities.

Additionally, DoT has participated in efforts to expedite compliance with existing international standards and to develop additional standards to enhance port, vessel, and facility security. DoT is also working with the U.S. Customs Service to implement the *Container Security Initiative* to ensure the security of the shipping supply chain. Shippers who do not comply with outlined rules and regulations will be subject to greater scrutiny and delays when entering U.S. ports.

Additional maritime mode protection initiatives include efforts to:

Identify vulnerabilities, interdependencies, best practices, and remediation requirements

DHS and DoT will undertake or facilitate additional security assessments to identify vulnerabilities and interdependencies, enable the sharing of share best practices, and issue guidance or recommendations on appropriate mitigation strategies.

Develop a plan for implementing security measures corresponding to varying threat levels

DHS and DoT will work closely with other appropriate federal departments and agencies, port security committees, and private-sector owners and operators to develop or facilitate the establishment of security plans to minimize security risks to ports, vessels, and other critical maritime facilities.

Develop processes to enhance maritime domain awareness and gain international cooperation

DHS and DoT will work closely with other appropriate federal departments and agencies, port security committees, and port owners and operators, foreign governments, international organizations,

and commercial firms to establish a means for identifying potential threats at ports of embarkation and monitor identified vessels, cargo, and passengers en route to the U.S.

Develop a template for improving physical and operational port security

DHS and DoT will collaborate with appropriate federal departments and agencies and port owners and operators to develop a template for improving physical and operational port security. A list of possible guidelines will include workforce identification measures, enhanced port-facility designs, vessel hardening plans, standards for international container seals, guidance for the research and development of noninvasive security and monitoring systems for cargo and ships, real-time and trace-back capability information for containers, prescreening processes for high-risk containers, and recovery plans. Activities will include reviewing the best practices of other countries.

Develop security and protection guidelines and technologies for cargo and passenger ships

DHS and DoT will work with international maritime organizations and industry to study and develop appropriate guidelines and technology requirements for the security of cargo and passenger ships.

Improve waterway security

DHS and DoT, working with state and local government owners and operators, will develop guidelines and identify needed support for improving security of waterways, such as developing electronic monitoring systems for waterway traffic; modeling shipping systems to identify and protect critical components; and identifying requirements and procedures for periodic waterway patrols.

MASS TRANSIT SYSTEMS

Each year passengers take approximately 9.5 billion trips on public transit. In fact, mass transit carries more passengers in a single day than air or rail transportation. If the effect on air transportation resulting from the September 11 attacks is an indicator, then a terrorist attack on a major mass transit system could have a significant regional and national economic impact.

Mass transit systems are designed to be publicly accessible. Most are owned and operated by state and local agencies. A city relies on its mass transit system to serve a significant portion of its workforce in addition to being a means of evacuation in case of emergency. Protection of mass transit systems is, therefore, an important requirement.

Each city and region has a unique transit system, varying in size and design. No one security program or information sharing mechanism will fit all systems. Despite these differences, as a general rule, basic planning factors are relatively consistent from system to system.

Mass Transit Mode Initiatives

Since transit is localized and varies significantly in size and design from system to system, identifying critical guidelines and standards for planning is key to unifying mass transit security activities. Panels in the Transit Cooperative Research Program have recommended and are overseeing 10 research projects in the areas of prevention, mitigation, preparedness, and response. Their recommendations can provide additional input to the development of these planning areas.

Additional mass transit protection initiatives include efforts to:

Identify critical planning areas and develop appropriate guidelines and standards

> DHS, working closely with DoT and other federal, state, and local mass transit officials, will identify critical planning areas and develop appropriate guidelines and standards to protect mass transit systems. Such critical planning areas and guidelines include design and engineering standards for facilities and rail and bus vehicles; emergency guidance for operations staff; screening methods and training programs for operators; security planning oversight standards; mutual aid policies; and continuity of operations planning.

Identify protective impediments and implement security enhancements

> DHS, working closely with DoT and mode representatives, will review legal, legislative, and statutory regimes to develop an overall protective architecture for mass transit systems and to identify impediments to implementing needed security enhancements.

Work with other sectors to manage unique risks resulting from interdependencies

> DHS, in collaboration with DoT, will convene cross-sector working groups to develop models for integrating priorities and emergency response plans in the context of interdependencies between mass transit and other critical infrastructures.

Mass Transit Mode Challenges

Mass transit is regulated by various agencies. These agencies must communicate and work together effectively to allow transit to work as a system rather than in separate modes. Mass transit is funded and managed at the local level, and operated as a not-for-profit entity. The Federal Transit Authority has limited legislative authority to oversee the security planning and operations of transit systems.

Mass transit systems were designed for openness and ease of public access, which makes monitoring points of entry and exit difficult. Protecting them is also expensive. Transit authorities must have the financial resources to respond to emergencies and maintain adequate security levels to deter attacks over broad geographic areas. The cost of implementing new security requirements could result in significant financial consequences for the industry.

BANKING AND FINANCE

The banking and financial services sector infrastructure consists of a variety of physical structures, such as buildings and financial utilities, as well as human capital. Most of the industry's activities and operations take place in large commercial office buildings. Physical structures to be protected house retail or wholesale banking operations, financial markets, regulatory institutions, and physical repositories for documents and financial assets. Today's financial utilities, such as

payment and clearing and settlement systems, are primarily electronic, although some physical transfer of assets does still occur. The financial utilities infrastructure includes such electronic devices as computers, storage devices, and telecommunication networks. In addition to the sector's key physical components, many financial services employees have highly specialized skills and are, therefore, considered essential elements of the industry's critical infrastructure.

The financial industry also depends on continued public confidence and involvement to maintain normal operations. Financial institutions maintain only a small fraction of depositors' assets in cash on hand. If depositors and customers were to seek to withdraw their assets simultaneously, severe liquidity pressures would be placed on the financial system. With this in mind, federal safeguards are in place to prevent liquidity shortfalls. In times of crisis or disaster, maintaining public confidence demands that financial institutions, financial markets, and payment systems remain operational or that their operations can be quickly restored.

Additionally, in times of stress the Secretary of the Treasury, the Chairman of the Federal Reserve, and the Securities and Exchange Commission proactively address public confidence issues, as was done following the September 11 terrorist attacks. The Department of the Treasury and federal and state regulatory communities have developed emergency communications plans for the banking and finance sector.

With regard to retail financial services, physical assets are well distributed geographically throughout the industry. The sector's retail niche is characterized by a high degree of substitutability, which means that one type of payment mechanism or asset can be easily replaced with another during a short-term crisis. For example, in retail markets, consumers can make payments through cash, checks, or credit cards.

The banking and financial services industry is highly regulated and highly competitive. Industry professionals and government regulators regularly engage in identifying sector vulnerabilities and take appropriate protective measures, including sanctions for institutions that do not consistently meet standards.

Banking and Finance Sector Challenges

Like the other critical sectors, the banking and financial services sector relies on several critical infrastructure industries for continuity of operations, including electric power, transportation, and public safety services. The sector also specifically relies on computer networks and telecommunications systems to assure the availability of its services. The potential for disruption of these systems is an important concern. For example, the equity securities markets remained closed for four business days following September 11, not because any markets or market systems were inoperable, but because the telecommunications lines in lower Manhattan that connect key market participants were heavily damaged and could not be restored immediately. As a mitigation measure, financial institutions have made great strides to build redundancy and backup into their systems and operations.

Overlapping federal intelligence authorities involved in publicizing threat information cause confusion and duplication of effort for both industry and government. The Department of the Treasury organized the Financial and Banking Information Infrastructure Committee (FBIIC) as a standing committee of the PCIPB. The FBIIC comprises representatives from 13 federal and state financial regulatory agencies.[1] The FBIIC is currently working with the National Infrastructure Protection Center, the Financial Services ISAC (FS-ISAC), and the OHS to improve the information dissemination and sharing processes.

Banking and Finance Sector Initiatives

The attacks in New York City on September 11 showed that the financial services industry is highly resilient. The strong safeguards and back-up systems the industry had in place performed well. Since 1998, the sector has been working with the Department of the Treasury to organize itself to address the risks of the emerging threat environment, particularly cyber intrusions. It was also the first sector to establish an ISAC to share security-related information among members of the industry.

Major institutions in this sector continue to perform ongoing assessments of their security programs. After the September 11 attacks, the industry and its associations initiated lessons-learned reviews to identify corrective actions for the improvement of security and response and recovery programs, as well as to provide a forum for sharing best practices through their trade associations and other interdisciplinary groups. The sector as a whole, with the support of the Department of the Treasury, has also initiated a sector-wide risk review. In addition to sector-wide efforts, individual institutions have stepped up their investments because of their better understanding of the threat.

Additional banking and finance sector protection initiatives include efforts to:

Identify and address the risks of sector dependencies on electronic networks and telecommunications services

The financial services sector's reliance on information systems and networks has resulted in a number of concerns for the industry. The Department of the Treasury, in concert with DHS, will convene a working group consisting of representatives from the telecommunications and financial services sectors, as well as other federal agencies, to study and address the risks that arise from the sector's dependencies on electronic networks and telecommunications services.

Enhance the exchange of security-related information

DHS will work with the Department of Treasury, the FBIIC, and the FS-ISAC to improve federal government communications with sector members and streamline the mechanisms through which they exchange threat information on a daily basis as well as during an incident.

---

1   The FBIIC includes representatives of the federal and state financial regulatory agencies, including: the Commodity Futures Trading Commission, the Conference of State Bank Supervisors, the Federal Deposit Insurance Corporation, the Federal Housing Finance Board, the Federal Reserve Bank of New York, the Federal Reserve Board, the National Association of Insurance Commissioners, the National Credit Union Administration, the Office of the Comptroller of the Currency, the Office of Federal Housing Enterprise Oversight, the Offices of Homeland and Cyberspace Security, the Office of Thrift Supervision, and the Securities and Exchange Commission.

CHEMICAL INDUSTRY AND HAZARDOUS MATERIALS

The chemical sector provides products that are essential to the U.S. economy and standard of living. The industry manufactures products that are fundamental elements of other economic sectors. For example, it produces fertilizer for agriculture, chlorine for water purification, and polymers that create plastics from petroleum for innumerable household and industrial products. Additionally, more than $97 billion of the sector's products go to health care alone.

Currently, the chemical sector is the Nation's top exporter, accounting for 10 cents out of every dollar. The industry is also one of our country's most innovative. It earns one out of every seven patents issued in the U.S., a fact that enables our country to remain competitive in the international chemical market.

The sector itself is highly diverse in terms of company sizes and geographic dispersion. Its product and service-delivery system depends on raw materials, manufacturing plants and processes, and distribution systems, as well as research facilities and supporting infrastructure services, such as transportation and electricity products.

Public confidence is important to the continued economic robustness and operation of the chemical industry. Uncertainty regarding the safety of a product impacts producers as well as the commercial users of the product. With respect to process safety, numerous federal laws and regulations exist to reduce the likelihood of accidents that could result in harm to human health or the environment. However, there is currently no clear, unambiguous legal or regulatory authority at the federal level to help ensure comprehensive, uniform security standards for chemical facilities.

In addition to the economic consequences of a successful attack on this sector, there is also the potential of a threat to public health and safety.[1] Therefore, the need to reduce the sector's vulnerability to acts of terrorism is important to safeguard our economy and protect our citizens and the environment.

Chemical Industry and Hazardous Materials Sector Challenges

Assurance of supply is critical to downstream users of chemical products for various reasons. Many large municipal water works maintain only a few days supply of chlorine for disinfecting their water supplies. Agricultural chemicals, particularly fertilizers, must be applied in large volumes during very short time periods.

Some products cannot be transferred between transportation modes. Facilities with "just-in-time" delivery systems maintain fewer and smaller chemical stockpiles.

The industry's ability to protect and assure the quality of its own chemical stockpiles is also important. Because chemicals are vital to many applications, contamination of key chemical stocks could impact a wide range of other industries, thereby affecting public health and the economy. In addition to the risk of contamination at product storage facilities, many chemicals are also inherently hazardous and, therefore, represent potential risks to public health and safety in a malicious context. Improving security can be expensive,

but there are cost-effective steps that industry can take to reduce vulnerabilities. Unfortunately, the risk profiles of chemical plants differ tremendously because of differences in technologies, product mix, design, and processes. Therefore, no single, specific security regime would be appropriate or effective for all chemical facilities.

Many current statutes related to the handling of highly toxic substances were created decades ago and may no longer be effective for monitoring and controlling access to dangerous substances. For example, although licensed distributors of pesticides can only sell them to licensed purchasers, license requests, which are granted at the state level by county extension agents, are fairly easy to obtain. In addition, the basis for licensing varies from state to state.

As in most other industries, the chemical industry relies on the availability, continuity, and quality of service and supplies from other critical infrastructures. For example, the chemical industry is the Nation's third largest consumer of electricity. An assured supply of natural gas at competitive prices is another crucial resource for the sector.

Chemical Industry and Hazardous Materials Sector Initiatives

Currently, parts of the industry have taken positive, voluntary steps to protect sector infrastructure. For example, several trade associations have developed or are developing security codes[2] to help their members address the need to reduce vulnerabilities. These commendable efforts will make important contributions to protecting key elements of the chemical and hazardous materials infrastructure against terrorist attack. These efforts are in the early stages of implementation. However, it should be also noted that a significant percentage of companies that operate major hazardous chemical facilities do not abide by voluntary security codes developed by other parts of the industry.

Chemicals and hazardous materials sector protection initiatives include efforts to:

Promote enhanced site security
DHS, in concert with EPA, will work with Congress to enact legislation that would require certain chemical facilities, particularly those that maintain large quantities of hazardous chemicals in close proximity to population centers, to undertake vulnerability assessments and take reasonable steps to reduce the vulnerabilities identified.

Review current laws and regulations that pertain to the sale and distribution of pesticides and other highly toxic substances
EPA, in consultation with DHS and other federal, state, and local agencies, as well as with other appropriate stakeholders, will review current practices and existing statutory requirements on the distribution and sale of highly toxic pesticides and industrial chemicals. This process will help identify whether additional measures may be necessary to address security issues related to those substances.

Continue to develop the chemical ISAC and recruit sector constituents to participate
The purpose of the chemical sector's ISAC, which is in the early stages of development, is to facilitate advanced warnings on security threats and the sharing of other security-related data. DHS and EPA, in concert with chemical industry officials, will promote the ISAC concept within the sector in order to draw increased participation from the industry at large.

---

1   Specific chemical and hazardous materials facilities may fall within the definitional context of "key assets," however, their specific protection issues relate directly to the entire sector and are therefore discussed in this chapter.

2   For example, the American Chemistry Council's Responsible Care® Security Code of Management Practices.

POSTAL AND SHIPPING

Americans depend heavily on the postal and shipping sector. Each day, we place more than two-thirds of a billion pieces of mail into the U.S. postal system; and each day more than 300,000 city and rural postal carriers deliver that mail to more than 137 million delivery addresses nationwide. In all, the vast network operated by the United States Postal Service (USPS) consists of a headquarters in Washington, D.C., tens of thousands of postal facilities nationwide, and hundreds of thousands of official drop-box locations. USPS employs more than 749,000 full-time personnel in rural and urban locations across the country and generates more than $60 billion in revenues each year. Together, USPS and private-industry mailing and shipping revenues exceed $200 billion annually.

The postal system is highly dependent on and interconnected with other key infrastructure systems, especially the transportation system. USPS depends on a transportation fleet composed of both service-owned and contactor-operated vehicles and equipment. Mail also travels daily by commercial aircraft, truck, railroad,

and ship. Because of these dependencies, many key postal facilities are collocated with other transportation modalities at various points across the United States.

The expansiveness of the national postal facilities network presents a significant, direct protection challenge. Additionally, the size and pervasiveness of the system as a whole have important implications in terms of the potential secondary effects of a malicious attack. The Fall 2001 anthrax attacks underscore this concern. In addition to localized mail stoppages across the U.S., the tainted mail caused widespread anxiety that translated into significant economic impact.

Historically, the American public has placed great trust, confidence, and reliance on the integrity of the postal sector. This trust and confidence are at risk when the public considers the mail service to be a potential threat to its health and safety. Consequently, USPS continues to focus on the specific protection issues facing its sector and is working diligently to find appropriate solutions to increase postal security without hampering its ability to provide fast, reliable mail service.

Postal and Shipping Sector Challenges

The protection challenges and initiatives discussed in this section relate specifically to the efforts undertaken by USPS. Commercial postal and shipping companies are in the process of organizing themselves as a sector to identify and address specific protection issues within their industry. While the USPS has worked with many of these companies to address critical infrastructure protection issues, there is further work to be done in this area. Assisted by USPS, DHS will engage the industry's major players in an effective dialogue to address critical infrastructure protection issues that cross the entire sector.

USPS has identified five areas of concern for the postal system:

- Points of entry and locations of key facilities;
- The mail's chain of custody;
- Unique constitutional and legal issues;
- Interagency coordination; and
- The ability to respond in emergency situations.

The fact that there are numerous points of entry into the postal system complicates its protection. Compounding this problem is the fact that these access points are geographically dispersed, including the multitude of postal drop boxes nationwide. Effective, affordable technology to scan mail and provide early warning of potential hazards is under current evaluation.

The location of many key postal service facilities can also aggravate risk-management challenges. Several major USPS facilities are collocated with or adjacent to other government agencies or major transportation hubs. Relocating these facilities to mitigate risk is often constrained by limited resources, a lack of available, alternative sites, and other pressing local imperatives.

Another factor affecting postal security is the fact that USPS does not always maintain control of the mail during its entire chain of custody. Oftentimes, independent contractors transport mail for USPS. Because USPS utilizes hundreds of long-haul mail carriers, mail moves into and out of USPS control along its route. To address this issue, USPS transportation purchasing requirements call for all transportation vendors, their employees, and subcontractors to submit to criminal and drug background checks. These checks include fingerprinting and follow-up if necessary by the Postal Inspection Service.

USPS security efforts face constitutional and legal challenges that are unique to the postal and shipping sector. Specifically, the Fourth-Amendment prohibition of unreasonable search and seizure and the sanctity of the postal seal make it necessary to justify the scanning or x-ray of a parcel for hazardous materials. Regardless, some technology vendors resist developing or marketing advanced sensing equipment out of concern that they would be held liable if their device failed to detect an actual threat. The *Support Anti-terrorism by Fostering Effective Technologies (SAFETY) Act*, enacted as part of the *Homeland Security Act of 2002*, reduces these risks by providing strong product liability protection for manufacturers of anti-terrorism devices.

Ensuring that USPS is able to respond effectively in emergency situations is another challenge for the sector. While USPS has worked extensively with vendors and the White House Office of Science and Technology Policy to develop solutions, currently there is no recognized set of standards to guide USPS and the private shipping industry in evaluating products for detecting, decontaminating, and remediating the effects of certain hazards. Furthermore, there are inadequate stockpiles of equipment and materials to enable sustained response activities. For instance, the supply of chemicals used to decontaminate facilities affected by the Fall 2001 anthrax incidents depended on a few companies, each of which produces only one of the compound's constituent parts.

In responding to the anthrax incidents, USPS worked with various federal agencies and state and local governments and continues to coordinate and plan with these groups. Further coordination and planning will be necessary to ensure that protection measures developed are effective across the entire sector. The federal authority to implement certain protective and response measures related to the actual or potential transmission of certain biological agents across state lines is not widely understood. Resolving these ambiguities in advance of a crisis situation would contribute greatly to the coordination of protection and emergency response efforts.

Postal and Shipping Sector Initiatives

DHS will work with private shipping and mail firms to enable them to incorporate their protection issues into a more comprehensive approach to critical infrastructure protection for this sector.

Additionally, the USPS has outlined six core initiatives in its emergency preparedness plans: prevention; protection and health-risk reduction; detection and identification; intervention; decontamination; and investigation. Specific key action areas that support these initiatives include efforts to:

Improve protection and response capabilities

DHS and USPS will conduct planning to increase reserve stockpiles of equipment and materials needed for emergency-incident response, particularly for CBR contaminants. They will also review requirements for manufacturing surge capacity for certain materials.

DHS and USPS will also work with other federal agencies and state and local authorities to facilitate coordinated planning efforts to develop and implement risk avoidance and reduction measures, as well as to establish common protocols for incident response and remediation.

Assure security of international mail

DHS and USPS will work with other appropriate agencies to clarify and formalize responsibilities for assuring the security of mail transiting U.S. borders, both inbound and outbound (e.g., between the USPS and U.S. Customs Service).

Promote and support ISAC participation

DHS will promote the postal and shipping sector's participation within an appropriate information sharing structure. This structure must include key government- and private-sector stakeholders involved with the delivery of air and ground mail, private parcels, and heavy cargo.

Conduct enhanced risk analyses of key facilities

DHS, USPS, and U.S. Postal Inspection Service will conduct assessments of postal facilities that are collocated with other high-risk facilities requiring more thorough risk analyses. These more rigorous assessments, which must take into account terrorist capabilities and motivations and facility vulnerabilities, will provide both indications and justification for the relocation of high-risk USPS facilities.

Improve customer identification and correlation with their mail

USPS will implement customer identification and correlation mechanisms at designated mail intake points and improve passive, nonintrusive parcel inspections for the detection of hazardous material.

Identify conflicts with respect to coordinated multi-jurisdictional responses

DHS, USPS, and DOJ will work together with state and local governments to identify and address conflicts in federal, state, and local laws and regulations that impair the abilities of multi-jurisdictional entities, like the USPS, to respond effectively in emergency situations.

PROTECTING KEY ASSETS

Key assets represent a broad array of unique facilities, sites, and structures whose disruption or destruction could have significant consequences across multiple dimensions. One category of key assets comprises the diverse array of national monuments, symbols, and icons that represent our Nation's heritage, traditions and values, and political power. They include a wide variety of sites and structures, such as prominent historical attractions, monuments, cultural icons, and centers of government and commerce. The sites and structures that make up this key asset category typically draw large amounts of tourism and frequent media attention—factors that impose additional protection challenges.

Another category of key assets includes facilities and structures that represent our national economic power and technological advancement. Many of them house significant amounts of hazardous materials, fuels, and chemical catalysts that enable important production and processing functions. Disruption of these facilities could have significant impact on public health and safety, public confidence, and the economy.

A third category of key assets includes such structures as prominent commercial centers, office buildings, and sports stadiums, where large numbers of people regularly congregate to conduct business or personal transactions, shop, or enjoy a recreational pastime.

Given the national-level fame of these sites and facilities and the potential human consequences that could result from their attack, protecting them is important in terms of both preventing fatalities and preserving public confidence.

NATIONAL MONUMENTS AND ICONS

National Monument and Icon Challenges

Our national monuments and icons present specific challenges because their protection typically combines the authorities, responsibilities, and resources of federal, state, and local jurisdictions, and, in some cases, private foundations. A clear division of labor, resources, and accountability is often difficult to distinguish.

The need to protect our national icons and monuments from terrorist attack requires the development and coordination of comprehensive policies, practices, and protective measures. We are also faced with the task of balancing open visitor access to these structures with the protection of visitors and the structures themselves. Most often their protection entails restricting public access to certain areas and curtailing, or even prohibiting, the assembly of large numbers of visitors.

The Department of the Interior (DOI) is the lead federal department with primary jurisdiction over national icons and monuments. It has diverse responsibilities, including the protection of a number of potential targets. Such protection is particularly important in the case of icons and symbols that figure prominently in national celebrations and events.

Accordingly, DOI must coordinate with law enforcement agencies across jurisdictions and entities directly responsible for intelligence gathering and homeland security.

DOI and its state, local, and private sector counterparts also face unique challenges with respect to recruiting, training, and retaining a robust security force. Given the need for the physical protection of such a wide array of potential targets (e.g., national parks, monuments, and historic buildings), maintaining a highly trained security force is a priority.

National Monument and Icon Initiatives

To address the challenges associated with the protection of our national monuments and icons, we will take action in the following areas:

Define criticality criteria for national monuments, icons, and symbols

> DOI will work in concert with DHS to develop specific guidance to define criteria and standards for determining the criticalities and protection priorities for our national monuments, icons, and symbols.

Conduct threat and vulnerability assessments

DOI will work in concert with DHS and other appropriate authorities to conduct threat and vulnerability assessments to identify gaps in visitor protection processes as well as asset protection.

Retain a quality security force

DOI will explore alternatives to foster efforts to recruit, train, and retain a skilled and motivated security force.

Conduct security-focused public outreach and awareness programs

DOI will enlist public support in the protection of our national icons and symbols through sustained public outreach and awareness programs.

Collaborate with state and local governments and private foundations to assure the protection of symbols and icons outside the federal domain

DOI will work with state and local governments and private institutions to explore alternatives to protect symbols and icons such as historical buildings and landmarks that are outside the purview of the federal government.

Evaluate innovative technologies

DOI, in concert with DHS and other key stakeholders, will explore ways to employ security technologies to ensure the protection of visitors to monuments and other like attractions.

Make provisions for extra security during high-profile events

DOI will work with law enforcement agencies to manage visitor periods at national monuments and provide extra security during high-profile events taking place in or around national icons.

NUCLEAR POWER PLANTS

Nuclear power represents about 20 percent of our Nation's electrical generation capacity. The U.S. has 104 commercial nuclear reactors in 31 states. For 25 years, federal regulations have required that these facilities maintain rigorous security programs to withstand an attack of specified adversary strength and capability. Nuclear power plants are also among the most physically hardened structures in the country, designed to withstand extreme events such as hurricanes, tornadoes, and earthquakes. Their reinforced engineering design provides inherent protection through such features as robust containment buildings, redundant safety systems, and sheltered spent fuel storage facilities.

The security at nuclear power plants has been enhanced significantly in the aftermath of the September 11 attacks. All plants remain at heightened states of readiness, and specific measures have been implemented to enhance physical security and to prevent and mitigate the effects of a deliberate release of radioactive materials. Steps have been taken to enhance surveillance, provide for more restricted site access, and improve coordination with law enforcement and military authorities. In addition to these augmented security measures, all nuclear power plants have robust security and emergency response plans in place to further assure public health and safety in the unlikely event of a malicious act and/or radioactive release.

Nuclear Power Plant Challenges

Losing the capabilities of a single nuclear power plant may have only a minor impact on overall electricity delivery within the context of our robust national power grid. Nevertheless, a terrorist attack on any nuclear facility would be considered a significant security event. In an unlikely worst-case scenario, a successful terrorist strike against a nuclear facility could result in a release of radioactive material. Even if radioactive material were not released, widely held misconceptions of the potential consequences of an

attack on a nuclear facility could have significant negative impact.

NRC is currently performing a detailed design basis threat and vulnerability analysis for nuclear power plants to help identify additional security enhancements that may be warranted. Additional prudent measures should be examined to help strengthen the defensive posture of these facilities.

Nuclear Power Plant Initiatives

To overcome protection challenges, we will:

Coordinate efforts to perform standardized vulnerability and risk assessments

NRC and DHS will work with owners and operators of nuclear power plants to develop a standard methodology for conducting vulnerability and risk assessments.

Establish common processes and identify resources needed to augment security at nuclear power plants

The NRC and DHS will work in concert with plant owners and operators and appropriate local, state, and federal authorities to develop a standard process for requesting external security augmentation at nuclear power plants during heightened periods of alert and in the event of an imminent threat.

Criminalize the carrying of unauthorized weapons or explosives into nuclear facilities

NRC, in coordination with DHS, will pursue legislation to make the act of carrying an unauthorized weapon or explosive into a nuclear power plant a federal crime.

Enhance the capabilities of nuclear power plant security forces

NRC, in coordination with DHS, will pursue legislation authorizing security guards at licensed facilities to carry and use more powerful weapons. It will also assist the industry to develop standards and

implement additional training in counter-terrorist techniques for private security forces.

Seek legislation to apply sabotage laws to nuclear facilities

NRC, in coordination with DHS, will pursue legislation to make federal prohibitions on sabotage applicable to nuclear facilities and their operations.

Enhance public outreach and awareness

NRC and DHS will work with plant owners and operators and appropriate local and state authorities to enhance public outreach and awareness programs and emergency preparedness programs.

DAMS

Some of our larger and more symbolic dams are major components of other critical infrastructure systems that provide water and electricity to large populations, cities, and agricultural complexes. There are approximately 80,000 dam facilities identified in the National Inventory of Dams. Most are small, and their failure would not result in significant property damage or loss of life. The federal government is responsible for roughly 10 percent of the dams whose failure could cause significant property damage or have public health and safety consequences. The remaining critical dams belong to state or local governments, utilities, and corporate or private owners.

Dam Challenges

Under current policies and laws, dam owners are largely responsible for the safety and security of their own structures. Hence, the resources available to protect dam property vary greatly from one category to the next. Additionally, the distributed nature of dam ownership also complicates assessment of the potential consequences of dam failure for certain categories of dams. Given these realities, the need to develop more comprehensive mechanisms for assessing and managing risks to dams is clear.

Dam Initiatives

To overcome protective challenges for dam structures, we will take action to:

Develop risk assessment methodologies for dams

DHS, in cooperation appropriate federal, state, and local government representatives and private-sector dam owners will design risk assessment methodologies for dams and develop criteria to prioritize the dams in the National Inventory to identify structures requiring enhanced security evaluations and protection focus.

Develop protective action plans

DHS, together with other appropriate departments and agencies, will establish an intergovernmental working group to explore appropriate protective actions for the Nation's critical dams.

Establish a sector-ISAC

DHS will work with other appropriate public and private sector entities to establish an information and warning structure for dams similar to the ISAC model in use within other critical infrastructure sectors.

Institute a national dam security program

DHS and other appropriate departments and agencies, such as the Association of State Dam Safety Officials and United States Society of Dams, will collaborate to establish a nationwide security program for dams.

Develop emergency action plans

DHS, together with other appropriate departments and agencies, will identify the areas downstream from critical dams that could be affected by dam failure and develop appropriate population and infrastructure protection and emergency action plans.

Develop technology to provide protective solutions

DHS, together with other appropriate departments and agencies, will explore new protective technology solutions for dams. Technology solutions hold significant promise for the identification and mitigation of waterborne threats. For example, technical options might include deploying sensors, barriers and communications systems to reduce the possibility of an unauthorized craft or device entering a critical zone located near a navigational dam.

GOVERNMENT FACILITIES

Before the September 11 attacks, the principal threat to government buildings was the use of explosives. After the 1995 bombing of the Alfred P. Murrah Building in Oklahoma City, the operators of many large government centers across the country implemented enhanced measures, such as concrete barriers, intensified surveillance, and parking restrictions, to safeguard key physical assets. While explosives remain an important concern, the innovative, highly coordinated Al-Qaeda attacks have added new dimensions to the threats now facing U.S. government facilities.

The General Services Administration (GSA) is a principal agency responsible for the management of federal government facilities. Additional departments and agencies are similarly involved in the management of federally owned or operated facilities, including DoD and the Department of Veterans Affairs. Within the overall federal inventory are buildings that the federal government owns and others that it leases from the private sector. GSA works with other federal agencies to conduct facility security assessments to ensure that each facility owned or leased by GSA identifies vulnerabilities to specific types of threats. The Federal Protective Service, which will transition into DHS, works with government tenants and private-sector owners to identify credible threats and implement appropriate countermeasures to provide cost-effective security.

Government Facilities Challenges

Most government organizations occupy buildings that are also used by a variety of nongovernmental tenants, such as shops and restaurants where the public is able to move about freely. In federally owned buildings, federal laws and regulations apply. In private facilities with federal tenants, federal laws and regulations only apply in areas that are federally occupied. For instance, federal laws and regulations prohibit the entry into federal buildings of prohibited weapons. In buildings where the federal government leases space, the weapons ban is applicable only to those spaces occupied by the federal tenants. Private owners of these properties may not want or have the ability to modify their procedures to accommodate the increased or special security countermeasures required by their federal tenants, such as installing surveillance cameras in lobbies, redesigning entry points to restrict the flow of traffic, or setting up x-ray machines and metal detectors at entrances. The need to consider the delicate balance between security and the public's right to privacy presents additional challenges.

Government Facilities Initiatives

To overcome protection challenges associated with government facilities, we will:

Develop a process to screen nonfederal tenants and visitors entering private-sector facilities that house federal organizations

DHS, together with GSA and other federal departments and agencies, will work with real-estate associations in the private sector to implement a noninvasive screening process at facilities that house private businesses as well as federal organizations.

Determine the criticality and vulnerability of government facilities

DHS, together with GSA and other federal departments and agencies, will work with owners of federally occupied facilities to establish a standard methodology to determine a government facility's criticality and vulnerability to facilitate security-related planning.

Develop long-term construction standards for facilities requiring specialized security measures

NIST, together with DHS and other federal government departments and agencies, will continue current efforts to develop long-term construction design standards for facilities requiring blast resistance or other specialized security measures.

Implement new technological security measures at federally occupied facilities

DHS, together with GSA and other federal departments and agencies, will work with owners of federally occupied facilities to explore measures to enhance security measures in the common areas of federally occupied facilities (e.g., sensor systems in lieu of manual-access control).

COMMERCIAL KEY ASSETS

Protecting prominent commercial centers, office buildings, sports stadiums, theme parks, and other sites where large numbers of people congregate to pursue business activities, conduct personal commercial transactions, or enjoy recreational pastimes presents significant challenges. Day-to-day protection of such facilities is the responsibility of their commercial owners and operators, in close cooperation with local law enforcement.

The federal government's responsibility for the protection of these assets is more or less indirect. Its activities include providing timely threat indications and warnings and working with commercial enterprises to harmonize individual facility security processes with the various Homeland Security Advisory System levels of alert. Additionally, providing support and input to organizations that develop standards and guidance for building construction and facility heating, ventilating, and air conditioning (HVAC) systems constitutes an important federal government activity.

The federal government typically coordinates or provides physical security at commercial facilities only in conjunction with dignitary visits or designated National Security Special Events. Given the national-level visibility and potential human and economic consequences of prominent commercial sites and facilities, it is important for the government and commercial sectors to work together to assure the protection of our nation's prominent business centers and gathering places.

Commercial Key Asset Challenges

The likelihood of terrorists targeting and attacking any specific, prominent commercial facility or activity is difficult to determine. Potential terrorist attack methods range from conventional explosives to CBR weapons of mass destruction. Each facility's vulnerability to the various means by which terrorists could strike is unique as determined by its engineering design, size, age, purpose, and number of inhabitants. Standards for building design, construction, and security also vary widely across enterprises, industrial sectors, and governmental jurisdictions. For the most part, commercial owners and operators must be responsible for assessing and mitigating their specific facility vulnerabilities and practicing prudent risk management and mitigating measures.

Commercial Key Asset Initiatives

There are no specific actions that will eliminate all of the potential risks associated with the threat of a determined terrorist attack on a prominent commercial facility or activity. However, there are certain steps that can be taken to reduce a facility's attractiveness as a target by complicating attack planning and execution, and helping to mitigate the effects of an explosive attack or CBR release.

For example, reducing a commercial facility's vulnerability to a high explosive or CBR attack requires a comprehensive approach. The first step is to integrate considerations for potential threats into the engineering design of the facility and its supporting systems (e.g., HVAC systems).

The second step is a thorough assessment of physical-security design features, systems, processes, and procedures that serve to deny or limit terrorist access to a facility and its key nodes. Preventing terrorist access to a targeted facility requires adequate physical security for all entrances, storage areas, maintenance areas, and rooftops, as well as securing access to the outdoor air intakes of facility HVAC systems.

The third step is an interior assessment of HVAC systems and their components. Specifically, this measure focuses on their vulnerability as conduits for the introduction and dispersal of CBR agents. Key areas considered during this assessment include HVAC system controls, airflow patterns, overpressure, purge capability, filtering efficiency, and leakage potential. If designed, installed, and maintained properly, air filtration and cleaning systems can mitigate the effects of CBR agents by removing contaminants from a facility's airborne environment.

A final step involves developing and rehearsing facility contingency plans based on scenarios involving the most likely and worst-case physical security breaches, aircraft impact, conventional explosive detonation, and CBR release scenarios. This final and important measure must include establishing processes and systems for coordinating and cooperating with local law enforcement and emergency response personnel.

To facilitate the protection of prominent commercial sites and facilities against terrorist attack, we will take action to:

Share federal building security standards and practices with the private sector

DHS, together with GSA, NIST and other federal departments and agencies will develop a program to share federal building protection standards,

vulnerability and risk assessment methodologies, best practices, and technology solutions (e.g. physical barriers, closed-circuit television, intrusion detection devices, CBR detection sensors, and explosive detection systems) with commercial facility owners and operators.

Facilitate efficient dissemination of threat information

DHS, in concert with the intelligence and law enforcement communities, will explore processes and systems to enable the timely dissemination of threat indications and warning information to commercial facility owners and operators.

Implement the Homeland Security Advisory System

DHS will collaborate with commercial facility owners and operators to align the Homeland Security Advisory System with specific measures and procedures pertinent to commercial facility security.

Explore options for incentives for the implementation of enhanced design features or security measures

DHS will explore options to facilitate incentives for commercial owners and operators who incorporate specific security and safety features into their facility design, or who adopt specific processes, procedures, and technologies that serve to deter, prevent, or mitigate the consequences of terrorist attacks.

Improve building codes for privately owned facilities

NIST will develop a comprehensive set of building codes for privately owned facilities designed to better assure structural integrity, minimize probability of collapse, and increase resistance to high-temperature fires.

CONCLUSION

Protecting our county's critical infrastructures and key assets is a core homeland security mission. This *Strategy* reaffirms our commitment as a Nation to protect our critical infrastructures and key assets against further terrorist attacks.

As we begin to address the myriad of physical protection challenges, we must keep in mind the complex nature of the infrastructures and assets we aim to protect. As a potential target set, our country's critical infrastructures and key assets are a highly diverse, interdependent mix of facilities, systems, and functions. Government owns and operates some of them. Most, however, are controlled by the private sector. All are vulnerable in some way to the terrorist threat.

They also represent a true "system of systems." Failure in one asset or infrastructure can cascade to disruption or failure in others, and the combined effect could prompt far-reaching consequences affecting government, the economy, public health and safety, national

security, and public confidence. As a whole, our protection mindset must include a thorough appreciation of these complexities as we carry out this national strategy for action.

In this document we have highlighted the diverse physical protection challenges that we face as a Nation. We have laid out a comprehensive agenda that will allow us to address the most pressing impediments to our physical protection based upon the prudent management of threats, vulnerabilities, and risks. This is only the beginning, however, of a long and challenging journey.

As we begin, we must also keep in mind the nature of the adversary we now face. The September 11 attacks on the World Trade Center and the Pentagon highlight our national-level physical vulnerability to the threat posed by a highly adaptive, patient, cunning, and flexible enemy. The attacks also demonstrate the extent of our

enemy's determination and sophistication, and the lengths to which terrorists will go to further their causes.

We no longer assume that terrorists are incapable of undertaking a devastating physical attack on our homeland and infrastructure base. In fact, given the creative and adaptive nature of our terrorist adversaries, we can expect future strikes to be even more sophisticated in terms of capability and synchronization. Ironically, the very nature of our free society greatly enables terrorist operations and tactics, while, at the same time, hinders our ability to predict or prevent terrorist acts or mitigate their effects. Given these realities, the imperative to implement the comprehensive national physical protection strategy outlined in this document is most pressing.

The issues and enabling initiatives outlined in the *Cross-Sector Security Priorities* chapter of this document represent important near-term national priorities. They focus on impediments to physical protection that significantly impact multiple key sectors of our government, society, and economy. Potential solutions to the challenges identified—such as information sharing and threat indications and warning—are high-leverage areas that, when realized, will enhance the Nation's overall ability to protect critical infrastructures and key assets across the board.

These action areas, which include the prompt identification and protection of nationally critical infrastructures and development of processes and systems to properly warn and protect specifically threatened assets will be the focus of the federal government's near-term critical infrastructure and key asset protection effort. Accordingly, DHS and designated federal lead departments and agencies will prepare detailed implementation plans to support the cross-sector and sector-specific priorities outlined in this document.

As we work to refine and implement our priority protection initiatives, we must bear in mind the guiding principles set forth in this document. First and foremost, our efforts must assure public health and safety, critical services, and public confidence in our government and economy. To accomplish this, we must establish clear roles and responsibilities, accountability, and coordinating structures and processes that will govern the interaction of all stakeholders.

We must also build and foster a partnership among all levels of government, as well as between government and the private sector. This public-private partnership should be based on a commitment to a two-way communications flow and the timely exchange of information relevant to critical infrastructure and key asset protection. This partnership should also extend to the research, development, and fielding of advanced technology solutions to common protection problems. Collaborative efforts should also include the development and sharing of modeling and simulation capabilities to enable public-private sector decision support and interdependency analysis.

Terrorists do not respect international boundaries and are, therefore, not restricted by them. Hence, we must extend our infrastructure and key asset protection partnership to include our Mexican and Canadian neighbors, as well as other friendly nations around the globe. Finally, as we take action to overcome the major impediments to our physical protection, we must take care to safeguard the fundamental constitutional freedoms that have long been the hallmark of this great Nation.

Federal departments and agencies, state and local government, and private sector owners and operators have made great strides to enhance the security of the critical infrastructures and key assets they respectively control. An intense cooperative spirit and tremendous sense of urgency have characterized our national domestic protection environment in the aftermath of the terrorist strikes of September 11. We have come a long way, but much work remains. We must act together now—through aggressive leadership at all levels inside and outside government—to build on this shared cooperative spirit and carry out the implementing activities endorsed in this document.

Our desired end state is the protection of our most nationally critical infrastructures and assets; timely warning and protection of those infrastructures and assets that face a specific, imminent threat; and a collaborative environment in which all stakeholders can effectively and efficiently carry out their respective protection responsibilities. Make no mistake—the road ahead will be fraught with challenges. Unified in our approach, however, we will overcome these challenges and secure our critical infrastructures and key assets from terrorist exploitation.

ACRONYMS

CBR: Chemical, Biological, or Radiological

DHS: Department of Homeland Security

DoD: Department of Defense

DoE: Department of Energy

DoI: Department of the Interior

DoJ: Department of Justice

DoS: Department of State

DoT: Department of Transportation

EMS: Emergency Medical Service

EPA: Environmental Protection Agency

FBIIC: Financial and Banking Information Infrastructure Committee

FCC: Federal Communications Commission

FERC: Federal Energy Regulatory Commission

FS-ISAC: Financial Services Information Sharing and Analysis Center

GSA: General Services Administration

HHS: Department of Health and Human Services

HVAC: Heating, Ventilating, and Air Conditioning

ISAC: Information Sharing and Analysis Center

ISP: Internet Service Provider

NERC: North American Electric Reliability Council

NGN: Next Generation Network

NIST: National Institute of Science and Technology

NOC: Network Operation Center

NRC: Nuclear Regulatory Commission

OHS: Office of Homeland Security

PCIPB: President's Critical Infrastructure Protection Board

PSTN: Public Switched Telecommunications Networks

R&D: Research and Development

USDA: United States Department of Agriculture

USPS: United States Postal Service